D1474516

THE ESSENTIAL GUIDE TO
FOUNDATIONS

FROM THE EDITORS OF

JLC
The Journal of Light
Construction

hanley▲wood

THE ESSENTIAL GUIDE TO
FOUNDATIONS

Published by Hanley Wood
One Thomas Circle, NW, Suite 600
Washington, DC 20005

Distribution Center
29333 Lorie Lane
Wixom, Michigan 48393

THE JOURNAL OF LIGHT CONSTRUCTION
186 Allen Brook Lane
Williston, Vermont 05495

Edited by Clayton DeKorne
Illustrations by Tim Healey
Production by Theresa Emerson
For more information on The Journal of Light Construction or to subscribe to the magazine, visit www.jlconline.com

HANLEY WOOD CONSUMER GROUP
Group Publisher, **Andrew Schultz**
Associate Publisher, Editorial Development, **Jennifer Pearce**
Managing Editor, **Hannah McCann**
Senior Editor, **Nate Ewell**
Proofreader, **Joe Gladziszewski**
Vice President, Retail Sales, **Scott Hill**
National Sales Manager, **Bruce Holmes**

Most Hanley Wood titles are available at quantity discounts with bulk purchases for educational, business,
or sales promotional use. For information, please contact Bruce Holmes at bholmes@hanleywood.com.

VC GRAPHICS
President, Creative Director, **Veronica Claro Vannoy**
Graphic Designer, **Jennifer Gerstein**
Graphic Designer, **Denise Reiffenstein**

10 9 8 7 6 5 4 3 2 1

Printed in the United States of America

Library of Congress Control Number: 2005932290

ISBN-10: 1-931131-50-3
ISBN-13: 978-1-931131-50-6

DISCLAIMER OF LIABILITY
Construction is inherently dangerous work and should be undertaken only by trained building professionals. This book is intended for
expert building professionals who are competent to evaluate the information provided and who accept full responsibility for the
application of this information. The techniques, practices, and tools described herein may or may not meet current safety requirements in
your jurisdiction. The editors and publisher do not approve of the violation of any safety regulations and urge readers to follow
all current codes and regulations as well as commonsense safety practices. An individual who uses the information contained in this
book thereby accepts the risks inherent in such use and accepts the disclaimer of liability contained herein.

The editors and publisher hereby fully disclaim liability to any and all parties for any loss, and do not assume any liability whatsoever
for any loss or alleged damages caused by the use or interpretation of the information found in this book, regardless of whether
such information contains deficiencies, errors, or omission, and regardless of whether such deficiencies, errors, or omissions result
from negligence, accident, or any other cause that may be attributed to the editors or publisher.

Acknowledgements

Several years ago, then Journal of Light Construction chief editor Steve Bliss assembled a group of editors to share thoughts on creating our own manual of best practice — the JLC Field Guide. We imagined this as a builder's trusty companion, ever present on the seat of the truck or in the toolbox, ready to answer the kinds of questions that come up on the job site every day.

Thanks to Steve Bliss, who envisioned, mapped, and directed the project in its early stages; to Clayton DeKorne, who expertly executed the work that Steve had started; to Tim Healey for illustration; to JLC staff editors Ted Cushman and Charlie Wardell, who compiled large portions of the original manuscript; to Josie Masterson-Glen for editorial production and copyediting; to Jacinta Monniere for the original book design; to Barb Nevins, Lyn Hoffelt, and Theresa Emerson for production work; to Ursula Jones for production support; and to Sal Alfano and Rick Strachan of Hanley Wood's Washington, D.C., office for executive management.

Finally, special thanks to all the authors and JLC editors over the years, too numerous to mention, whose work is the basis of this volume.

Don Jackson
JLC Editor

Introduction

Over the last 20 years, The Journal of Light Construction has amassed a wealth of first-hand, practical building knowledge from professionals who have dedicated themselves to custom residential projects. In the Home Building & Remodeling Basics Series, we have distilled this valuable knowledge into handy reference guides — selecting the critical data, fundamental principles, and rules of thumb that apply to strategic phases of residential building and remodeling.

Our intention is not to set building standards, but to provide the housebuilding trades with a compilation of practical details and proven methods that work for the many builders, remodelers, subcontractors, engineers, and architects who are committed to producing top-quality, custom homes. The recommendations we have compiled in these volumes usually exceed the building code. Code compliance is essential to building a safe home — one that won't collapse or create unsafe living conditions for the occupants. However, we are striving to reach beyond this minimum standard by offering a record of best practice for residential construction: details and methods used not only to produce a safe building, but to create a long-lasting, fine-quality home.

While it is not our first focus, we have made every effort to uphold the building codes. The prescriptive recommendations in this book are generally consistent with the 2000 International Residential Code and the Wood Frame Construction Manual for One- and Two-Family Dwellings, published by the American Forest and Paper Association. Although these standards reflect the major U.S. model codes (CABO, BOCA, ICBO, and SBCCI), regional conditions have forced some municipalities to adopt more stringent requirements. Before taking the information in this volume as gospel, consult your local code authority.

As comprehensive as we have tried to make this resource, it will be imperfect. Certainly we have strived to limit any error. However, many variables, not just codes, affect local building and remodeling practices. Climate variability, material availability, land-use regulations, and native building traditions all impact how houses are built in each city, town, county, and region. To account for every variation would require a database of understanding far greater than the scope of this book. Instead, we focus here on some principles of physics, design, and craftsmanship that won't change by region or style. It is our hope that these principles, used alongside the building code, will guide professionals toward a greater understanding of best practice.

Clayton DeKorne

Editor

How to Use this Book

This volume is intended to be used as a reference book for professionals and experienced homeowners with an understanding of basic construction techniques. It is organized in general order of construction, and within each section we have provided several navigational tools to help you quickly located the information you need, including a section headline at the top of the page, cross-references within the text, and references to Figures and illustrations.

Table of Contents: The two-page table of contents found on the following spread offers a detailed look at this book — featuring not just each section, but the individual topics found therein, along with page numbers for quick reference.

Index: A detailed index of the entire volume can be found at the back of this book.

Figures: When appropriate, tables, graphs, and illustrations have been added to help clarify the subject matter. Every effort has been made to place these Figures on the same page, or spread of pages, as the copy which references them. You will find references to Figures in bold in the text; in the event that the Figure falls on an earlier page or in another section, a page reference will be included in the text.

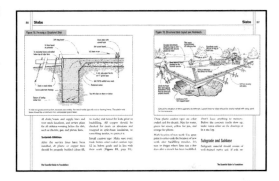

Be sure to pick up the other three books in the Home Building & Remodeling Basics Series for more valuable information that will help you get your next project done right:

• The Essential Guide to Framing
• The Essential Guide to Exteriors
• The Essential Guide to Roofing

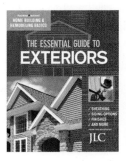
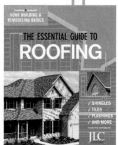

Table of Contents

Concrete Block Foundations

Permanent Wood Foundations

Retaining Walls

Slabs

Pier Foundations

Waterproofing and Dampproofing

Drainage

Backfill

Insulation

Radon Abatement

Estimating

Estimating Sitework

Costs of sitework depend on particular soil and site conditions (see "Evaluating Soils on Site," page 6). Unseen soil conditions below grade can drastically increase sitework costs and change design requirements. (Complications and issues are explained in greater detail in the "Soil" and "Sitework" sections of this chapter.)

Estimating Earth Removal

When calculating earth removal volumes, the volume of dirt is always much larger than expected. Dirt becomes entrained with air as you dig and swells in volume; double the volume of *embankment earth* to find the volume of *loose yardage*. Calculate sloped embankments as shown in **Figure 1**.

When pricing excavation and fill, include these factors:

* **Hauling Charges**
  Hauling is often the biggest cost of fill materials, and travel time can also boost excavators' and other operators' fees.

Figure 1. Estimating Earthwork

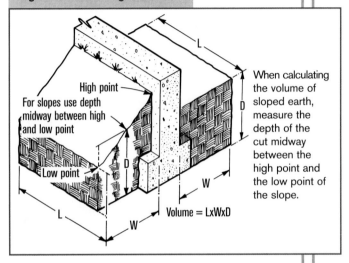

High point
For slopes use depth midway between high and low point

Low point

When calculating the volume of sloped earth, measure the depth of the cut midway between the high point and the low point of the slope.

Volume = LxWxD

* **Disposal Charges**
  Costs of disposal for removed earth and rock vary by locale.

Estimating Concrete

Concrete subcontractors often charge a unit rate per yard of concrete, especially for flatwork. Use **Figure 2** to calculate total yards of concrete.

Use a 5% to 10% waste factor to cover subgrade irregularities or spillage. If pouring trenched footings, overdigging in the trench cannot be filled with soil, so allow for extra concrete.

Figure 2. Coverage of One Cu. Yd. Concrete

WALL AREA (SQ. FT.) = WALL HT. x WALL LENGTH
SLAB AREA (SQ. FT.) = SLAB LENGTH x SLAB WIDTH
YDS. OF CONCRETE = AREA x COVERAGE

Thickness of Wall or Slab (in.)	Coverage (sq. ft./yd.)
12	27
11	$29\frac{1}{2}$
10	32
9	36
8	40
7	46
6	54
5	65
4	81
$3\frac{1}{2}$	93
3	108
$2\frac{1}{2}$	130
2	162

To calculate the concrete yardage required for a foundation wall or slab, first calculate the wall or slab area, then multiply by the coverage factor (column 2 for each given thickness).

Figure 3. Concrete Amounts for Piers and Pier Footings

Round Pier Footing Diameter	Concrete Amt. per Pier	80-lb. Bags Concrete Mix
8-in.	.013 cu. yd.	0.6 bags per ft.
10-in.	.02 cu. yd.	0.9 bags per ft.
12-in.	.029 cu. yd.	1.3 bags per ft.

Rectangular Pier Footing Dimensions	Concrete Amt. per Footing Unit	80-lb. Bags Concrete Mix
8x16x16-in.	.044 cu. yd.	2 bags
10x20x20-in.	.086 cu. yd.	3.8 bags
12x24x24-in.	.15 cu. yd.	6.75 bags

Estimating Concrete for Piers

Figure the amount of concrete needed to fill a sonotube by multiplying the height of the tube in feet by the concrete amount per pier, as shown in **Figure 3**.

Estimating Block

To estimate standard 8x16-in. block:

1 SQUARE FT. OF WALL = 1.125 BLOCK

WALL AREA (SQ. FT.) x 1.125 = TOTAL BLOCK NEEDED

(Note: When using 8-in. block, convert all wall and opening heights and lengths to multiples of 8 in.)

Estimating Mortar

When mixing mortar, allow one bag of masonry cement for every 28 block:

TOTAL BLOCK NEEDED ÷ 28 = BAGS CEMENT NEEDED

Allow one ton of sand for each 8 bags of masonry cement:

TOTAL BAGS OF MASONRY CEMENT NEEDED ÷ 8 = TONS OF SAND NEEDED

Mortar Batches

When setting block, expect to use about one batch of mortar per 100 block. When using mortar to set and parge, allow one batch per 60 block.

Soils

Good natural soils can support almost any residential foundation. However, problem soils can contribute to moisture problems, settlement, building movement, or foundation failure. Soil problems can turn up after construction has begun. When work starts, stay alert to soil conditions that may affect schedules or could cause damage to work in progress — especially subsidence, erosion, frost action, or drainage problems.

Soil Types

Different soil types are classified mostly by the size of the soil particles (**Figure 4**).

Most soils are blends of different particle sizes, and so they have combined names such as "silty sand" or "clayey gravel."

Characteristics of Soil Types

Different soils have different characteristics that make them more or less

Figure 4. Soil Types	
Soil Type	**Particle Size (fractions of in.)**
Gravel	Larger than $1/5$
Coarse Sand	$1/5$ to $8/100$
Fine-Medium Sand	$3/1,000$ to $8/100$
Silt	$3/1,000$ to $4/10,000$
Clay	Smaller than $4/10,000$

Different soil classification systems use different particle sizes to define soil types. Approximate values shown here are drawn from the Unified Soil Classification System. To determine particle sizes, samples are sifted through a series of screen with different mesh sizes.

suitable as a support for a foundation or as a well-draining backfill. Refer to **Figure 5**.

Bearing Capacity of Soils

If the native soil type is known, codes allow builders to assume a bearing strength based on soil type (**Figure 6**). Footings must be placed on undisturbed original soil to use these assumed values. Soil testing may

Figure 5. Properties of Soils According to the Unified Soil Classification System

Unified Soil Classification System Symbol	Soil Description	Drainage Characteristics	Frost Heave Potential	Volume Change Potential (Expansion)
Soil Group I				
GW	Well-graded gravels, gravel-sand mixtures, little or no fines	Good	Low	Low
GP	Poorly graded gravels or gravel-sand mixture, little or no fines	Good	Low	Low
SW	Well-graded sands, gravelly sands, little or no fines	Good	Low	Low
SP	Poorly graded sands or gravelly sands, little or no fines	Good	Low	Low
GM	Silty gravels, gravel-sand mixtures	Good	Medium	Low
SM	Silty sand, sand-silt mixtures	Good	Medium	Low
Soil Group II				
GC	Clayey gravels, gravel-sand-clay mixtures	Medium	Medium	Low
SC	Clayey sands, sand-clay mixtures	Medium	Medium	Low
ML	Inorganic silts and very fine sands, rock flour, silty or clayey fine sands or clayey silts with slight plasticity	Medium	High	Low
CL	Inorganic clays of low to medium plasticity, gravelly clays, sandy clays, silty clays, lean clays	Medium	Medium	Medium to Low
Soil Group III				
CH	Inorganic clays of high plasticity, fat clays	Poor	Medium	High
MH	Inorganic silts, micaceous or diatomaceous fine sandy or silty soils, elastic silts	Poor	High	High
Soil Group IV				
OL	Organic silts and organic silty clays of low plasticity	Poor	Medium	Medium
OH	Organic clays of medium to high plasticity, organic silts	Unsatisfactory	Medium	High
PT	Peat and other highly organic soils	Unsatisfactory	Medium	High

Note: The percolation rate for good drainage is over 4 in. per hour; medium drainage is 2- to 4-in. per hour; and poor drainage is less than 2 in. per hour.

The table above shows the two-letter designations for the soil types defined in the Unified Soil Classification System, which is widely used for construction engineering. A soil engineering report will usually use this scheme to identify soils on a site. In general, sands and gravels have good characteristics for bearing strength and drainage, while soils that contain more fine silt or clay are weaker and drain more slowly. Soils that contain large amounts of decaying plant material (the peats and organic clays) are no good for building and have to be removed.

establish higher bearing strengths, in which case footing size sometimes can be reduced.

To support foundation loads, the width of the footing depends on the loadbearing value of the soil. See "Footings," page 44.

Soil Pressure on Foundations

Pressure exerted by soil on the sides of foundation and basement walls is a major concern in the design and construction of foundation walls (**Figure 7**) and retaining walls. This is known as *lateral pressure*, and is defined in terms of *equivalent fluid pressure*. Similar to the way water pressure increases at increased depth, lateral soil pressure increases with depth of soil (or height of fill).

Water in soil tends to increase lateral pressure:

- Silts and clays (especially clays) become more fluid-like as they become wet or saturated, exerting greater lateral pressure than they do when dry.

> **Caution**
> In any soil, the risk of sudden trench collapse or foundation failure may increase as soils become saturated.

Figure 6. Soil Bearing Capacities

Material	Loadbearing Value (pounds per sq. ft.)
Crystalline bedrock	12,000 psf
Sedimentary rock	4,000 psf
Sandy gravel or gravel	3,000 psf
Sand, silty sand, clayey sand, silty gravel, and clayey gravel	2,000 psf
Clay, sandy clay, silty clay, and clayey silt	1,500 psf

Loadbearing values indicate the amount of force that undisturbed, native soils can support. Refer to **Figure 38**, page 44 for sizing concrete and masonry footings.

2000 International Residential Code

- Sands and gravels tend to be less influenced by water content.

Equivalent Fluid Pressure

Soil pressures are usually the greatest loads on a foundation. Code rules of thumb can be used when building on sites with natural sand or gravel soils. Engineered design is recommended when natural soils are clay or silt.

As a rule of thumb, code assumes a lateral fluid pressure of 30 psf for block or concrete foundations, which is typical for a well-drained sand or gravel soil. But fine, cohesive soils can exert higher pressures. **Figure 8** shows typical fluid pressures associated with various soil types in different foundation cases.

Look for foundation soils that exert low pressures in the active and at-rest cases, and exert high resistance in the passive case. Sand and gravel meet these requirements. By contrast, soft clays — which exert high pressures in the active and at rest cases and are relatively weak in the passive case — are not good foundation soils. Foundation and retaining wall failure is a much greater threat when the structure is built on clay.

Soil Drainage

Coarse soils drain better than fine soils. The ability to drain is measured by a *permeability coefficient* (**Figure 9**). The higher the coefficient, the better a soil can drain.

Evaluating Soils on Site

It is hard to identify soils precisely in the field. If you are uncertain about the soil type, consult a soil engineer. A preliminary soil investigation may give enough information to go on, but sometimes an engineering soils report will be required.

Soil Identification

Some rough information about soils can be learned from simple on-site tests:

Common Soil Terms

A few terms that may crop up in soil reports are defined here:

Cohesiveness. Soils that stick together when dry are called cohesive. Very fine-grained soils (clays and some silts) are cohesive soils. When dry, they solidify into a firm mass, but as water is added they soften and then become liquid.

Noncohesive or cohesionless soils. These are also called granular soils because of their large particle size and grainy shape. Granular soils include gravels and sands, as well as some silts. Granular soils are generally stronger and better-draining than cohesive soils.

Plasticity. As clays and some silts go from a dry to a wet state, they go through a state that is neither solid nor liquid – a soft and workable condition called the plastic state. Soils that are plastic through a high range of water contents are called highly plastic soils, or are said to have high plasticity. Highly plastic soils have low bearing strengths and exert a lot of pressure on foundation walls.

Gradation. The range or distribution of particle sizes in a soil is called gradation or grading. A gravel or sand with even amounts of different pebble or particle sizes will be called "well graded," while a soil with mostly one particle size or with one particle size missing will be called "poorly graded" or "gap graded."

Problem Soils

Organic soils. Soils containing decaying plant or animal matter, like topsoil or peat, are a special type called organic soils. Organic soils will not support a building and should be removed, or the building must be relocated.

Expansive clay. Certain clays that are highly attractive to water tend to expand with force when wet and shrink when dry; this is a special class of soil called expansive clay. Expansive soil swells when it gets wet and shrinks when it dries, leaving large cracks that channel water down into the hillside. The swelling action of expansive soil can be powerful enough to lift a house, and expansive soil used for perimeter fill can cause windows and doors to stick, and stucco, siding, drywall, and even the foundation to crack. A site with expansive soil may require specialized pier and grade beam foundations with extensive drainage, deeper piers and footings, and more heavily reinforced concrete slabs (see "Pier Foundations," page 97). In many cases, the expansive soil must be removed and replaced with non-expansive fill.

Natural fill vs. engineered fill. Soils that have been moved or brought in from outside, called fill, are not a soil type as such, but may be any type of soil that's been moved to a new location. Fill often contains junk, debris, or wood and tree stumps. Because it subsides, compresses, and washes out, fill is generally unsafe to build on. The only exception is engineered fill, or soil material that has been carefully placed and compacted under an engineer's supervision.

Figure 7. Lateral Pressure on Foundations

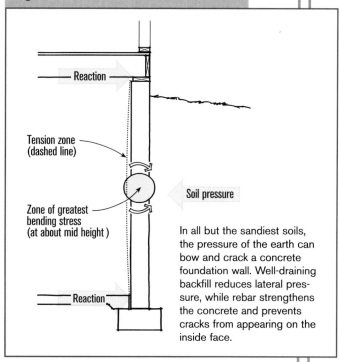

Reaction

Tension zone (dashed line)

Zone of greatest bending stress (at about mid height)

Soil pressure

Reaction

In all but the sandiest soils, the pressure of the earth can bow and crack a concrete foundation wall. Well-draining backfill reduces lateral pressure, while rebar strengthens the concrete and prevents cracks from appearing on the inside face.

- **Dirt-ball test:** To assess soil cohesiveness, take a moist double handful of soil and squeeze it into a ball, then drop it from a height of about 1 foot. If the soil will not form a ball or if the ball readily fragments when dropped, the soil is relatively non-cohesive and granular, with a low proportion of fine clay. However, if the soil forms a ball that holds together when dropped, it is more likely to contain a high percentage of cohesive clay.

- **Water suspension test:** Drop a scoop of soil into a large jar of water. Gravel and sand will settle to the bottom of the jar almost

Figure 8 Soil Fluid Pressures

Soil Classification	Friction Angle (degrees)	Density or Consistency	Unit Soil Weight (pcf)	Equivalent Fluid Pressure (psf/ft. of depth)		
				Active	At Rest	Passive
Course sand or	45	compact	140	24	41	820
sand and gravel	38	firm	120	29	46	510
	32	loose	90	28	42	290
Medium sand	40	compact	130	28	46	600
	34	firm	110	31	48	390
	30	loose	90	30	45	270
Fine sand	34	compact	130	37	57	460
	30	firm	100	33	50	300
	28	loose	85	31	41	280
Fine, silty sand	32	compact	130	40	61	420
or sandy silt	30	firm	100	33	50	300
	28	loose	85	31	45	280
Fine, uniform	30	compact	135	45	68	400
sand	28	firm	110	38	58	300
	26	loose	85	33	48	220
Clay silt	20	medium	120	59	79	245
	20	soft	90	44	59	183
Silty clay	15	medium	120	84	99	170
	15	soft	90	53	67	153
Clay	10-0	medium	120	84-120	99-120	170-120
	10-0	soft	90	63-90	74-90	153-90

This chart shows estimated pressures exerted by various types of soils under three conditions. The **active** case refers to situations where the structure can give somewhat to relieve the pressure, such as a foundation restrained by a wood frame floor. The **at rest** case applies if the structure cannot flex at all, as when a foundation wall is pinned in place by a concrete slab. The **passive** case applies when the structure wants to move but the soil is resisting that force.

immediately. Finer silt particles will take fifteen minutes to an hour to settle. Clay particles will remain suspended in water for a day or longer. So if the water remains very cloudy for a long time, the soil probably contains a high percentage of clay.

- **Noodle test:** Roll a small quantity of soil into a thin noodle or string shape between your palms. If the soil can be rolled as thin as 1 in. without breaking apart, it is probably a cohesive soil with a substantial percentage of clay.

Caution

These casual tests are not a substitute for a soils laboratory report. Visual identification of soils is unreliable. For example, soils containing both clay and gravel may look like gravel but behave as clay. Soils containing 20% clay have the bearing strengths and drainage characteristics of a clay soil, and soils containing 30% clay are defined as clays even though large amounts of gravel may be present.

Soil Borings

The building department may require soil borings taken by a qualified geotechnical engineering firm. Even if not required, an engineer's report is useful to establish the type of soil, the bearing strength of the soil, lateral soil pressures, drainage characteristics of the site, and the presence of rock below the surface.

Figure 9. Permeability Rates in Soils

Soil	Permeability Coefficient
Fine to coarse, clean gravel	23 ft./min.
Uniform, fine gravel	11 ft./min.
Uniform, very coarse, clean sand	6.9 ft./min.
Uniform, coarse sand	1.0 ft./min.
Uniform, medium sand	14 ft./hr.
Clean, well-graded sand and gravel	1.4 ft./hr.
Uniform, fine sand	13 ft./day
Well-graded, silty sand and gravel	1.3 ft./day
Silty sand	9.8 ft./month
Sandy clay	5 ft./month
Silty clay	1.2 in./month
Clay	1.2 in./month

Brent Anderson Associates

- Soil borings, or "test pits," are recommended on low-lying sites near water, on sites that are suspected of having been filled in the past, or whenever soft, unstable, or expansive soils are encountered during excavation.

- Sample borings are especially important where piers are involved, because they help determine both the presence of water and the anticipated depth of the piers.

- A sample boring analysis can determine whether on-site soils will be useful as engineered fill.

Figure 10. Soil Pressure Beneath Footings

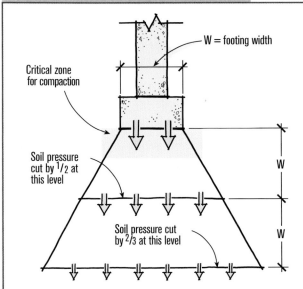

As the load under a footing spreads out, pressure on the soil diminishes. Soil directly under a footing takes the greatest load. To ensure against settlement, footing trenches should be thoroughly compacted.

Number of Borings

- On flat, well-drained sites, at least two test pits should be bored, at opposite corners of the proposed foundation. Intermediate borings may be required if the test holes are far apart. It is the site engineer's responsibility to determine if this is required.

- On hillsides or potentially wet sites, at least four or five borings should be taken, preferably on both the uphill and downhill sides of the proposed building.

Depth of Borings

- On flat, well-drained sites, borings should be made to a depth 5 to 8 ft. below the proposed footing depth.

- On hillsides, deep borings — 25 ft. deep or deeper — are essential. A deep boring can better define "bedrock" and help locate subterranean water moving horizontally through the hillside. A deep boring may also identify ancient landslides and waterways, which can affect the stability of the ground above.

Compacting Soil

Any fill that is placed during or after construction, and any soil that is disturbed during excavation, must be compacted to prevent future settlement.

- Compact footing trenches and slab sub-bases before pouring footings or adding a gravel base (**Figure 10**).

- Compact backfill in utility trenches to prevent settlement.

- Compact backfill around foundation walls.

- It is best to use a gravel or sandy gravel for fill, because the compaction of silts and clays is too hard to control.

Compacting Different Soil Types

Some soils are easier to compact than others (**Figure 11**). In general, gravel sub-bases can be quickly compacted with a vibrating plate compactor. Gravel used for backfill will settle very little, even if not compacted. By contrast, clays typically require engineering and may not be practical to compact at all.

Compacting Equipment

For gravels and sands, use a vibrating plate compactor or vibrating smooth roller. For silts, use a vibrating compactor or an impact compactor (jumping jack). For clays, use an impact compactor.

Compact Soil in Lifts

Place and compact soil in lifts no higher than 6 in.

Effect of Moisture on Compaction

Different soils compact best at different moisture contents. Moisture in a granular soil lubricates the grains and helps them slide into a more tightly packed arrangement. In cohesive soils, moisture makes the soil somewhat moldable. However, too much moisture in a soil will hold particles apart and prevent full compaction. On site, properly moistened soils will hold together in a ball when squeezed, but will not release water. To accurately specify and monitor optimum soil moisture, however, engineering services are required.

Compaction Engineering

Jobs with soil engineering specifications usually call for a minimum soil compaction as measured by the *Proctor test*. This lab test determines the optimum moisture content of a specific type of compacted soil. An engineer can then measure field compaction with a density meter; 90% of the lab value is considered sufficient.

Figure 11. Soil Compacting Characteristics

Type of Soil	Compacting Characteristics and Equipment
Gravel	Compacts readily with vibrating plate
Sand	Compacts well with vibrating plate
Silt	Can be compacted with difficulty; impact compactors work best
Clay	Difficult or impractical to compact (consult engineer)
Organic soil	Not compactible (do not use for building site)

Each type of soil responds best to a given type of compaction equipment. Any organic soil, such as topsoil or peat, cannot be compacted and should not be used.

Sitework

Site Preparation

Excavation must not begin until the locations of underground wires, cables, and pipes have been marked, or until you have verification from utility companies that the area is clear.

> **Caution**
> Look for existing utilities before any excavation begins. Any digging within 24 in. of utility locations must be done by hand.

Clearing the Site

Clear the site at least 20 to 25 ft. from the foundation. This involves more than cutting down the trees and pushing them into a pile with a bulldozer:

- Cut up trees and haul them way
- Chip the brush
- Remove the stumps and haul them away

Saving Topsoil

Retain as much topsoil as possible to preserve the environmental quality of a site. Topsoil helps maintain vegetation that will preserve the soil and limit erosion (see "Practical Erosion Control," page 17). When topsoil will be preserved, till the soil first, and then remove to a safe location with a front-end loader. On wooded sites, however, saving topsoil is often more difficult than it's worth because of the number of roots.

Excavating Slab Foundations

Foundation excavations should be as level as possible, particularly for structural slabs. Set an elevation benchmark prior to excavation. Place the benchmark somewhere convenient and make sure everybody on the site knows where it is during excavation.

Plan all utility layouts that will run beneath slabs prior to digging (see "Site Layout for Slab Foundations," page 87).

Excavating Foundation Holes

Plan foundation drainage before excavating to identify the locations of cleanouts and daylight drains (see "Drainage," page 105).

Overdig foundation holes to give plenty of room for a well-draining backfill (see "Soil Drainage," page 6), and to provide room to work.

- If the depth of the excavation is 6 ft. or less, overdig by 3- to 4-ft.

- If the excavation is deeper than 7 ft., the sides must be sloped outwards at a 45-degree angle above 4 ft. (**Figure 12**), or install shoring (**Figure 16**, page 17).

Excavating Hillsides

One of the problems with excavating steep sites is that as you dig into a hillside, you remove material that holds the hill together, creating an unstable and potentially dangerous situation.

Angle of Repose

Excavate the hill back to an angle of repose — the angle at which the slope is stable. Each type of soil has a natural

Figure 12. Open Excavations

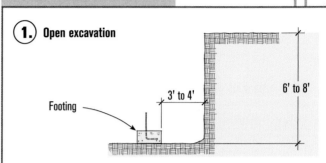
1. Open excavation
Footing — 3' to 4' — 6' to 8'

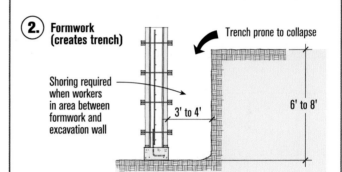
2. Formwork (creates trench)
Trench prone to collapse
Shoring required when workers in area between formwork and excavation wall
3' to 4' — 6' to 8'

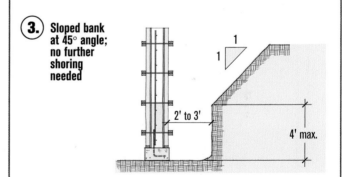
3. Sloped bank at 45° angle; no further shoring needed
1 / 1
2' to 3' — 4' max.

As the load under a footing spreads out, pressure on the soil diminishes. Soil directly under a footing takes the greatest load. To ensure against settlement, footing trenches should be thoroughly compacted.

Figure 13. Hillside Cuts

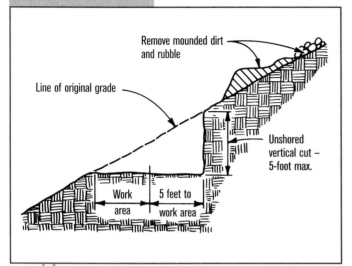

Remove mounded dirt and rubble

Line of original grade

Unshored vertical cut – 5-foot max.

Work area

5 feet to work area

Often, shoring is the only safe alternative and will eliminate worry about how delays, change orders, or bad weather will affect the hillside (see "Shoring," page 16).

Pressure Grouting

In porous soils, which are very much at risk of collapse, you may need to drill a pattern of small-diameter holes in the hillside and inject them with concrete. This kind of pressure grouting is expensive and is best left to an experienced specialty subcontractor.

angle of repose. For most soils it is usually safe to excavate back to a 2:1 slope. This is the easiest and least expensive way to stabilize a hillside, but it's often not practical on a single-family lot because there simply is not enough room.

Vertical Cuts vs. Shoring

An unshored vertical cut should not exceed 5 ft. on a sloped site (**Figure 13**). Be sure to reduce the danger of collapse by removing mounded dirt and rubble that can add a surcharge to the area above the cut. Install a series of steps or terraces — as required — to meet minimum height restrictions and reduce erosion (**Figure 14**).

Excavation Safety

An excavation collapse poses an extreme danger to workers. Soil is heavy —typically weighing more than 100 pounds per cu. ft. This means that a 3x3x3-ft. hole will contain 27 cu. ft. of soil that can weigh almost $1\frac{1}{2}$ tons as much as a car. If the soil is damp, wet, or filled with rock, it will weigh even more.

Excavation Failure

Keep an eye out for these signs of distress in and around trenches and open excavations:

- Cracks in the soil parallel to or in the face of an excavation

Caution in Frozen Ground

Frozen soil is as capable of collapsing as thawed soil of the same type, and should not be considered a safe alternative to proper shoring.

- Subsidence of the edge or bulging of the side of the excavation (this may be hard to see)

- Heaving or boiling of the bottom of the excavation, which is an indication of imminent failure

- Spalling or raveling of the face of the excavation (this probably indicates lack of proper sheeting and the lack of, or failure to, classify the soil)

- Water running into the excavation from the surface or face (do not allow workers in excavations with standing or running water)

- Bending, buckling, or groaning of any support member (if any movement of a support member can be seen or heard, an extremely dangerous situation exists)

Trench Safety Checklist

- The sides of trenches may need to be sloped back, depending on soil type and trench depth (**Figure 15**).

- Place excavated soil at least 2 ft. from the top edge of the trench, or position it behind a stable barrier.

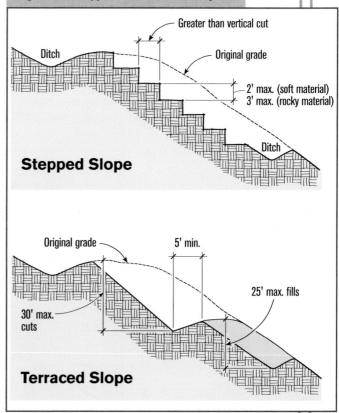

Figure 14. Stepped and Terraced Slopes

- Trenches more than 4 ft. deep should contain an exit ladder that extends at least 3 ft. above ground level and is located within 10 ft. of a worker at all times.

- Cross-braces and trench jacks should be level and spaced vertically in order to prevent wall material from moving into the trench (**Figure 16**).

- Trench boxes or safety cages can provide alternate protection methods.

Figure 15. Trenching Cuts

Stiff and firm soils (Types 1 & 2)

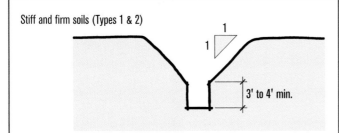

3' to 4' min.

Soils likely to crack and crumble (Type 3)

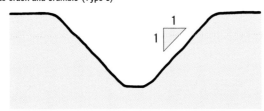

Soft and loose soils (Type 4)

Stiff and firm soils: For trenches deeper than 6 ft., slope sides back at a minimum 45-degree angle above 4 ft. **Soils likely to crack or crumble:** Slope entire height of trench side at a minimum 45-degree angle. **Soft and loose soils:** In sand, gravel, silt, organic soil, soft and wet clay, and loose fill, cut trench sides at a minimum 3:1 slope.

Shoring

In areas where vibrations or unstable conditions are likely, such as near a highway, railroad, or a backfilled trench, plan for very complete shoring.

Provide shoring in an open excavation (foundation hole) deeper than 7 ft. and in trenches deeper than 6 ft., unless the sides have been cut at a slope. On hillside sites, restrict unshored, vertical cuts to 5 ft. (see "Excavating Hillsides," page 13).

Installing Shoring

- When installing shoring, place the bucket of the excavation machine in the trench directly in front of the shoring being installed.

- When installing shoring struts or jacks, work from the top down, and remove struts working from the bottom up. Using this method, the worker is protected by the shoring already installed.

- Do not try to remove a jack under pressure or it may cause a sudden collapse. Backfill up to the bottom jack before it is removed; then up to the next jack and so forth.

Shoring Alternative

If shoring is not used, slope the walls of the excavations at a grade of 1:1 (45 degrees) or shallower (**Figure 12**, page 13). Foundation excavations should be sloped back anyway to provide room enough for a well-draining backfill.

Figure 16. Trench Shoring

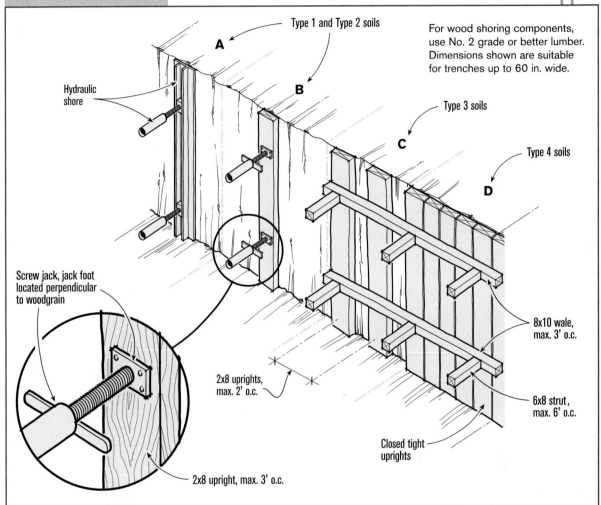

Type 1 and Type 2 soils

A

B

For wood shoring components, use No. 2 grade or better lumber. Dimensions shown are suitable for trenches up to 60 in. wide.

Type 3 soils

C

Type 4 soils

D

Hydraulic shore

Screw jack, jack foot located perpendicular to woodgrain

8x10 wale, max. 3' o.c.

2x8 uprights, max. 2' o.c.

6x8 strut, max. 6' o.c.

Closed tight uprights

2x8 upright, max. 3' o.c.

Practical Erosion Control

Cleared and excavated sites are prone to erosion from runoff that will carry silt and sand, which can pollute streams and wetlands or damage nearby properties. Fuel, pesticides, and other chemicals also may be carried into the environment by runoff. To avoid liability and reduce landscaping costs, take these practical steps to minimize erosion and pollution:

Preserve vegetation: Protect grass, trees, and other plants wherever possible. Maintain strips of grass or other growth across cleared slopes to catch water and soil runoff.

Figure 17. Temporary Construction Entrance

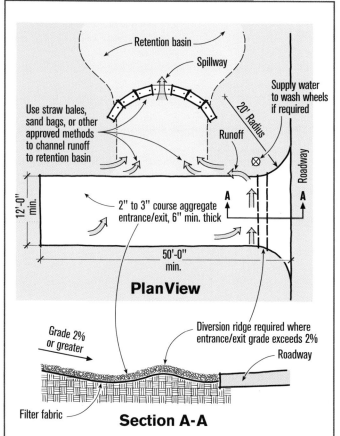

Retention basin

Spillway

Supply water to wash wheels if required

Use straw bales, sand bags, or other approved methods to channel runoff to retention basin

Runoff

20' Radius

Roadway

12'-0" min.

2" to 3" course aggregate entrance/exit, 6" min. thick

A — A

50'-0" min.

Plan View

Grade 2% or greater

Diversion ridge required where entrance/exit grade exceeds 2%

Roadway

Filter fabric

Section A-A

Drives should be installed before construction begins. If the schedule does not allow for this, use 2- to 3-in. of coarse gravel for a temporary roadbed, and use silt fences or straw-bales to trap silt and prevent erosion.

site — do not drive over uncleared areas. Protect uncleared areas with snow fencing or other barriers. Place barriers around the drip-line of trees to prevent injury to root systems. If a permanent drive cannot be installed before construction begins, a temporary gravel driveway should be installed where vehicles enter the job site (**Figure 17**).

Channel runoff: Divert runoff around cleared areas by mounding earth berms and digging swales. Where concentrated runoff encounters a cleared slope, create a lined channel or install a drain pipe at the bottom of a swale and cover with gravel. Make drain channels as long and gently sloped as practical. Seed low-volume, shallow swales with grass. Use fabric or rock to protect higher-volume channels.

Install silt barriers: Erect silt fences or staked hay-bale barriers on the downhill edge of disturbed earth slopes (**Figure 18**). Straw bales placed on slope contours should be tightly butted and staked to prevent erosion or flow between and under bales (**Figure 19**).

Protect drains and watercourses: Set up silt fences or staked hay-bale barriers around any stream, drainage

Schedule work in stages: Do not clear or excavate large areas too far in advance of construction; disturb vegetation only as needed, then reseed or replant as soon as is practical.

Control vehicle traffic: Limit equipment traffic in and out of the job

channel, or drain opening. Surround storm drains with straw-bale dikes to detain water so silt can settle out. If plans include new, permanent stormwater drainage, install the system as soon as possible, then protect inlets during construction.

Build sediment traps: Use sandbag and gravel structures or silt fencing to pond and detain runoff water, allowing sediment to settle out. Inspect sediment traps and excavate sediment as needed. Place excavated sediment in flat upland areas and seed immediately.

Preserve topsoil: Topsoil is necessary for reseeded plants to thrive (see "Saving Topsoil," page 12). If the existing topsoil will not support vegetation, import good soil. Topsoil is not suitable for use as backfill or subgrade.

Cover exposed soil: Reseed cleared areas as soon as possible. Seed soil (or excavated soil stockpiles) immediately if they will remain on the site for a period of time. If slopes or earth stockpiles cannot be reseeded immediately, cover with plastic sheeting (short-term only), mulch (heavy layer of wood chips or straw), or erosion-control fabric (mesh, netting, or geoblanket).

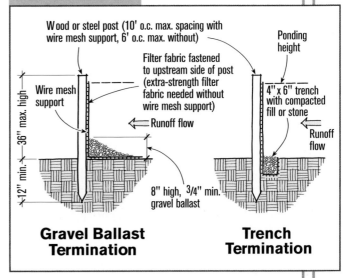

Figure 18. Silt Fence

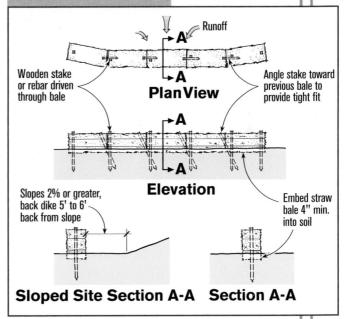

Figure 19. Straw-Bale Dike

Drives and Roadways

Driveway materials serve to spread out the load of vehicle traffic over a wider area. The main choices for residential driveways are gravel, asphalt, and concrete. For all three types of driveways, performance depends, in large part, on the quality of the subgrade.

Driveway Layout

Evaluate the drainage strategy for any drive at the layout stage (see "Subgrade Drainage," next page).

Driveway Width

Plan for a 12- to 14-ft.-wide roadbed. With a paved roadbed, you could get away with 11 ft., but some drivers might feel a little restricted on such a narrow drive, especially if it's long.

If you have two or three houses at the end of the driveway, with two-way traffic likely, you'll need to go with a 22-ft.-wide road.

Turnarounds

On a long driveway, plan for parking and a turnaround so residents don't have to back out. Don't skimp on space in a turnaround; the minimum turning radius should be 24 ft. to allow room for larger cars or pickup trucks.

Driveway Subgrade

- All driveway beds should be cut in stable native soils.
- Cut out soil or place fill to create the proper drainage grade.
- Plan the cut so the finished driveway is at least 1 in. higher than the surrounding soil.
- Clear the roadbed of roots, twigs, bushes, grass, and topsoil that will decay and might cause the drive surface to sink or break up.

Unsuitable Soils

Peat and expansive clays should be excavated and replaced with compacted granular fill. Unpaved drives built on soils with high clay content must be stabilized with lime (see "Subgrade Stabilization," page 25).

Existing Fill

On existing home sites, probe the soil with a steel rod. If resistance below the top 6 in. is less than resistance at the surface, deep fill may have been placed and compacted only at the surface, leaving an unreliable subgrade. Uncompacted fill should be excavated down to native soil and replaced with proper fill.

Subgrade Drainage

A subsurface drainage system consists of trenches, drainpipe, stone or gravel aggregate, and geotextiles (**Figure 20**). A complete system is crucial to keeping unpaved drives from turning to mud, and for extending the life of more expensive paved toppings.

Drainage Patterns

Grade the subsurface so it slopes away from the building site, if possible, to allow water from rain or snow-melt to drain away from the house.

Drainage for Downhill Drives

If the building site is at the bottom of a slope, build a swale to collect water, or use a slot drain in front of the garage door and wherever else the water might flow toward the building. Connect slot drains to a collection drain large enough to carry the water away from the building. If the drainage design might not completely handle all the water, plan on a step-up and ramp into the garage.

Drainage for Uphill Drives

On uphill driveways, route subsurface drainage to a storm sewer or ditch at the edge of the main road. On rural sites, the driveway usually passes over an entrance culvert where it intersects the main highway. Bring the drain pipe from your drain system to this collection point, so the ditch will carry away the run-off. Put a rodent screen over the drain pipe because field mice will damage polymeric materials.

Drainage Trenching

After grading the roadbed, excavate drainage trenches on both sides of the road. A small, 6-in.-wide chain trencher works best. The trenches should be at least as deep as the drain pipe or fin drain, but deeper is better.

Figure 20. Roadbed Construction

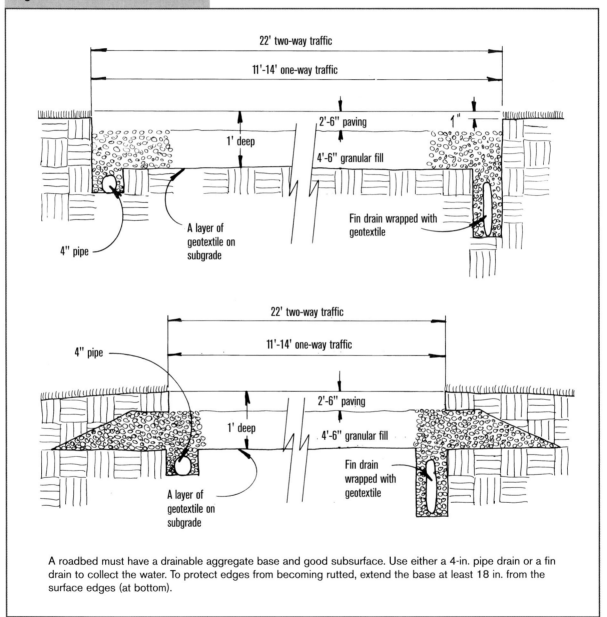

22' two-way traffic

11'-14' one-way traffic

2'-6" paving

1"

1' deep

4'-6" granular fill

Fin drain wrapped with geotextile

A layer of geotextile on subgrade

4" pipe

22' two-way traffic

11'-14' one-way traffic

4" pipe

2'-6" paving

1' deep

4'-6" granular fill

Fin drain wrapped with geotextile

A layer of geotextile on subgrade

A roadbed must have a drainable aggregate base and good subsurface. Use either a 4-in. pipe drain or a fin drain to collect the water. To protect edges from becoming rutted, extend the base at least 18 in. from the surface edges (at bottom).

Geotextiles

After grading subgrade, lay down a good "road fabric" — a minimum 20-mil woven polypropylene. Geotextile fabric actually provides tension support across the bottom of the base materials, allowing the road to carry greater loads. Without road fabric, wheel action will eventually push the granular base materials into the mud, creating potholes in paved surfaces and corrugations in unpaved surfaces.

Drainage Pipe

Lay the geotextile across the subgrade and drainage trenches, then lay in drainage pipe — a standard 4-in. corrugated drain tubing or fin drains. (Fin drains can carry more water; see "Drainage," page 105). Wrap geotextile around the drain.

Driveway Shoulders

On many driveways, the owners will want to landscape right up to the edge of the paving. The best way to handle this is to extend the road base 18- to 24-in. beyond the road surface, then haul in topsoil, spreading it over the shoulders of the base and right to the edges of the finish surface (**Figure 20**). This method will help stabilize the edges of the surface lift.

Figure 21. Road Mix

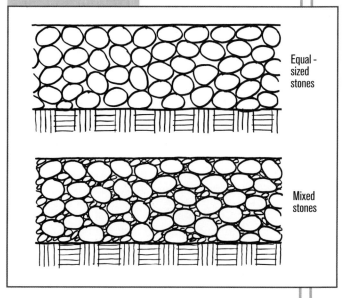

Equal-sized stones

Mixed stones

Driveway Base Materials

Good road base requires a mix of aggregate sizes (**Figure 21**). Avoid using pea gravel and other natural gravels from river deposits. These aggregates are too round and smooth, and will not compact well, so they are likely to shift under traffic.

Placing Base Materials

Firm compaction of base fill is crucial for any areas that will carry vehicle traffic. Place up to 12 in. of fill in at least two, 6-in. lifts. Compact each lift with the wheels of a tractor or with construction trucks, or compact with a

---

Base Materials for Unpaved Drives

The base material used for an unpaved drive is different than it is for paved roads, but good base and subgrade drainage material are important for both.

Road pack: A mix of gravel or crushed stone, road pack contains a high percentage of fine aggregate (called "fines"), and is the least expensive material used for unpaved drives. While road pack compacts well and is reasonably stable when dry, it has very poor internal drainage and gets soft and spongy when wet. Do not use in wet, low-lying areas. A roadbed made of this material should be graded several times a year to keep it from getting rough and to keep it free of potholes.

Open-graded aggregate: This is a gravel mix with particles ranging from about 1/4- to 1-in. in diameter (range of sizes in the mix varies according to local supplier), which will drain better than road pack, but is not stable enough to use as the surface course of a driveway.

Crushed stone: The best base material for a gravel drive is crushed stone, which is angular and compacts well, but doesn't clog as easily as road pack. The more angular the material, the less regrading will be required. Crushed stone mixes vary by region, and every region has its own numbering system for specifying aggregate.

---

small crawler (roller) from a rental yard. If the schedule allows, let the driveway sit for several months to allow settlement before placing a final 3- to 4-in. lift of surface fill (gravel drives) or paving with asphalt or concrete.

Wet-Site Roadbeds

When building a road over wetlands, do not cut and fill. Not only is digging messy and expensive, but it may be difficult to get permits. Land planners frown on any roadbed with deep gravel fill that might create a dam and block wetlands from flowing.

Lay road fabric over the ground, and place a layer of 3- to 5-in. stone on top of the road fabric to help spread out traffic loads on the soggy land (**Figure 22**). Over this stone, spread another layer of geotextile, and place 6- to 8-in. of mixed gravel base material, topped by a 3- to 4-in. layer of gravel surface mix.

Gravel Drives

Unpaved roads typically have the same surface and base materials (see "Base Materials for Unpaved Drives," above). Proper subgrade preparation, good subsurface drainage, and the use of geotextiles are critical for maintaining a drivable surface over time.

Subgrade Stabilization

Subgrade soil stabilization will help make an unpaved driveway less muddy and will help prevent potholes and corrugation. Use hydrated lime, distributed from open bags off the tailgate of a pickup truck. Add 3% to 5% by weight of the soil. Mix in the lime to a depth of 4- to 6-in. with a garden tiller or a disk; then recompact the subgrade.

Surface Mix for Unpaved Roads

After the house is finished and the last load of topsoil has been hauled onto the job site, top the road with a surface mix. This can be the same material used for the base, but good practice calls for 2- to 4-in. of a "three-quarter-minus" mix — 3/4-in. stones, fine stones, and a small amount of clay or organic topsoil for a binder. Alternatively, use 4 in. of 1/2-in. stone "plant mix," which has a complete mix of aggregate to create a smooth surface.

Place the surface mix in thin, 2-in. lifts, and compact each lift with a crawler.

Figure 22. Driveway Construction for Wet Sites

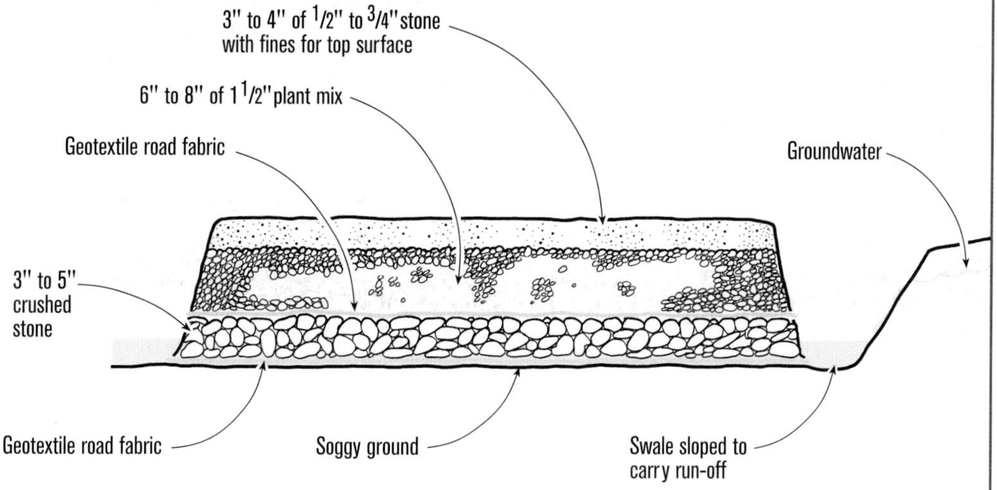

3" to 4" of 1/2" to 3/4" stone with fines for top surface
6" to 8" of 1 1/2" plant mix
Geotextile road fabric
Groundwater
3" to 5" crushed stone
Geotextile road fabric
Soggy ground
Swale sloped to carry run-off

On wet sites, place road fabric directly on top of soggy ground and cover with a heavy stone base. Next, install a second layer of fabric over the stone before placing the gravel base and surface layers.

The driveway surface should finish out to be at least 1 in. higher than the surrounding soil.

Asphalt Drives

An asphalt, or "blacktop," drive is the best system to use when you have a long approach to a home. Blacktop is a bitumenized concrete — a mixture of asphalt and small stones, 1/2 in. or smaller — that should last for 12 to 14 years. Eventually, asphalt will begin to lose its ability to expand and contract with temperature changes, and cracks will form. To prolong the life of the driveway, the owner should be prepared to fill cracks and put on a sealer coat every two years.

For asphalt drives, prepare subgrade and install subsurface drainage, as described on pages 20-24.

Base Materials for Asphalt Drives

The aggregate mix used for a paved road is slightly different from that used for an unpaved road. Because blacktop will spread loads better than a gravel surface, the base does not need to be as tightly packed. Larger chunks of aggregate will drain better, since there is plenty of room for water to percolate through and travel to the drains at the sides of the road.

Use 3/4- to 1-in. gravel as a base for asphalt. Compact the base materials with a plate compactor or vibratory roller. This material is harder to spread and compact than dense-grade base mix, such as road pack. If it will be left for a few months before paving, add some smaller aggregate — a mix of 1/8- to 3/8-in. angular aggregate — at the surface.

Base Thickness for an Asphalt Drive

Place a minimum of 6- to 8-in. of aggregate base material over the roadbed, as well as the drain system. A base thickness of 8- to 12-in. of gravel will extend the life of the blacktop; it's cheaper to put in more base material and less asphalt.

Asphalt Mix

Asphalt hot mix should have an asphalt/cement ratio of 4.5% to 6% by weight for the first lift (the *tack course*) and 5% to 7% for the *wearing course*.

Do not use cold-mix asphalt. This is used only for patching.

Placing Asphalt Paving

- Before applying blacktop, roll the base to ensure even compaction. If soft spots are detected, add fill and compact. Crown the base course slightly to the center of the driveway width (1- to 2-in. over 12 ft.). This ensures that when the topping is applied, the surface will drain and there will be no low spots where puddles can form.

- Some asphalt mixes may require a primer.

- Place asphalt on a warm day. Asphalt that cools too fast won't compact well. Do not place on frozen base materials.

- On a residential drive, asphalt can be placed in a single lift. However, it is better to apply it in two thin lifts, rolling between the tack course and the wearing course.

- With a 10- to 12-in. base, the total asphalt thickness can be as thin as $1^1/2$ in. For a 6- to 8-in. base, increase the topping thickness to about $2^1/2$ in.

- Apply the top, wearing course at one time so there are no seams in it. Roll it out until all roll marks disappear.

Figure 23. Concrete Driveway Construction

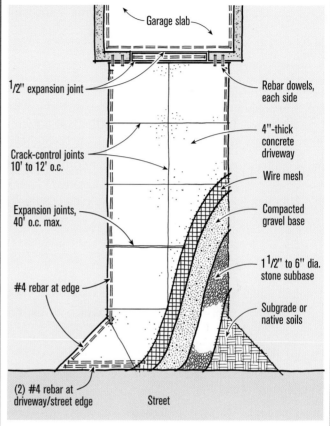

Garage slab

$^1/2$" expansion joint

Crack-control joints 10' to 12' o.c.

Expansion joints, 40' o.c. max.

#4 rebar at edge

(2) #4 rebar at driveway/street edge

Street

Rebar dowels, each side

4"-thick concrete driveway

Wire mesh

Compacted gravel base

$1^1/2$" to 6" dia. stone subbase

Subgrade or native soils

Plan View

To prevent settling and cracking, a concrete driveway must be built on a well-compacted base and subbase. Use rebar to reinforce slab edges and control joints to limit surface cracking.

Asphalt Edges

Edge reinforcing is typically not required, but you must compact soil well along the edges, or else the outer few inches will chip off (see "Driveway Shoulders," page 23). Cover the gravel base at the edge with geotextile, then sod or topsoil.

Concrete Driveways

Like other durable roadbeds, a concrete drive is built up in layers: A subgrade of native soil (if suitable) or compacted fill, a subbase of compacted stone, a base of compacted gravel, then a 4-in. concrete slab (**Figure 23**, page 27).

Subgrade and Subbase

Concrete is brittle and requires more support than a gravel or asphalt

topping. If the native soils are free-draining sand or gravel, they can be compacted to serve as a subbase. Otherwise, $1^1/2$-in. (maximum) stone should be brought in and compacted for the subbase.

Base Materials for Concrete Drives

Use a $3/4$- to 1-in. gravel as a base for concrete, placed and compacted as described for other roadbeds (see "Placing Base Materials," page 23).

Preparing Slab Edges

Because concrete is so brittle, slab edges can chip or break if they are thin or unsupported. Before pouring concrete, scrape the outermost corners of the form to clear build-up of loose soil so that the slab is full thickness (or thicker) and supported on a well-compacted subgrade.

Where the driveway joins the street, thicken the concrete to 12 in. and reinforce with double rebar (**Figure 24**).

Concrete for Driveways

Driveway surfaces may not see heavy truck traffic, but they may take a lot of

Figure 24. Concrete Driveway Subbase

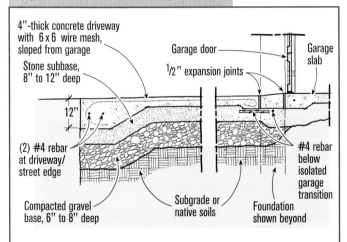

4"-thick concrete driveway with 6 x 6 wire mesh, sloped from garage

Stone subbase, 8" to 12" deep

Garage door

1/2" expansion joints

Garage slab

12"

(2) #4 rebar at driveway/ street edge

#4 rebar below isolated garage transition

Compacted gravel base, 6" to 8" deep

Subgrade or native soils

Foundation shown beyond

Concrete requires a subbase of compacted stone fill. The subbase adds support and serves as a capillary break for preventing frost heaves from cracking the brittle surface.

abuse from freeze-thaw cycles and road salt. Use a minimum 3,500-psi concrete mix with a maximum 4-in. slump (see "Concrete," page 30).

Isolation Joints

Concrete expands and contracts with temperature. To prevent damage to the driveway or other structures, place expansion joints where the driveway meets the street and the house, and within the driveway every 40 ft. or less (see "Control Joints," page 65).

Garage Transition

Where the driveway meets the garage, the driveway slab should be free to move up but not down. Even a piece of garage door trim that restrains the slab from heaving upward may crack the concrete. Expansion joints must also be placed on each side of a garage transition to isolate the driveway from the garage (**Figure 23**, page 27).

To support the slab edge and to keep it from sinking near the garage transition, drive rebar dowels into drilled holes in the foundation wall (#4 bar, 12-in.-long, driven minimum 2 in. into wall, 4 ft. o.c.).

Expansion joints in exterior slabs should be sealed with caulk to prevent water from infiltrating the joint (**Figure 89**, page 96).

Crack Control Joints

All concrete will crack from shrinkage as elements cool after placement and water evaporates. Control joints are provided to induce cracking to occur at the intended location. In driveways, place control joints in a roughly square grid with squares 10- to 12-ft. on a side. When cracks occur, seal the cracks with caulk. Advise homeowners that caulk must be renewed every few years to prevent water intrusion below the slab.

Crack Control Reinforcement

Support from the base, not from steel in the slab, gives the slab the strength to carry vehicle loads. Steel should be included to limit the size of shrinkage cracks. Use #3 or #4 rebar around the slab perimeter, 3 in. from the edge and 2 in. down from the top surface. In the field, use 6x6-in. welded wire mesh, 2 in. down from the top surface (**Figure 24**).

Concrete

Concrete is made up of Portland cement, water, air, and aggregate (sand and gravel). Depending on the mix, the rough proportions by volume are about 10% cement, 20% water and air, 30% sand, and 40% gravel (**Figure 25**).

Figure 25. Components of Concrete

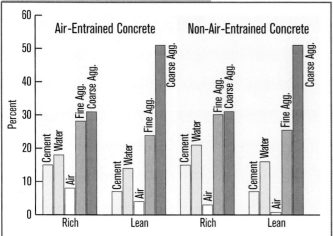

Percentages of cement, water, air, sand, and gravel in concrete mixes. Rich mixes contain higher percentages of cement. Air-entrainment introduces tiny air bubbles that allow the concrete to flow easier with less water, which makes for a stronger mix. The trapped bubbles also absorb minor expansion and contraction, allowing the concrete to better resist freeze/thaw damage.

Specifying Ready-Mix

Depending on the needs of the project, ready-mix suppliers can provide hundreds of different concrete mixes. In general, it's a good idea to tell your supplier what the concrete will be used for, and follow the supplier's recommendations for the appropriate mix. However, a builder should understand the way mix adjustments affect the concrete's properties.

At a minimum, concrete specifications will usually call out the compressive strength and water/cement ratio (**Figure 26**), as well as the slump (**Figure 29**, page 32). Concrete mixes can vary in the type and quantity of cement, the ratio of water to cement, the percentage of entrained air, and the size and grading of aggregates. You may also want to order concrete with various admixtures for special circumstances (see "Admixtures," page 33).

Cement Types

Figure 27 shows the five standard types of cement in use today.

Aggregate

Sand and gravel are the strongest and cheapest ingredients in concrete. It is most economical to use aggregate that is large and well-graded (containing a good proportion of various sizes from large to small), because this reduces the required volume of cement paste. If reinforcing steel will be spaced close together, or if concrete must be pumped, maximum gravel sizes may have to be reduced.

Using more fine sand makes a concrete mix "creamier" and makes it easier to achieve a smooth finish; however, the mix will require more water, and therefore should have more cement added for adequate strength.

Water

Water used to mix concrete should be clean enough to drink. Adding water to a concrete mix can weaken concrete. Follow water/cement ratio guidelines below.

Water/Cement Ratio

The ratio of water to cement should be strictly controlled to ensure that the concrete reaches the specified strength

Figure 26. Selecting Residential Concrete

Structural Element	Minimum Compressive Strength Required	Practical Water/Cement Ratios
Foundations, basement walls, and slabs not exposed to weather	2,500– 3,000 psi	.55
Foundations, basement walls, and slabs exposed to weather	3,500 psi	.45
Driveways, garage slabs, sidewalks, porches, patios, and steps exposed to weather	3,500– 4,000 psi	.45

Figure 27. Types of Cement

Type	Use
Type I, Type IA (air-entraining)	Good for most residential work
Type II, Type IIA (air-entraining)	Use where soils and ground water contain moderate sulfates that can attack concrete
Type III, Type IIIA (air-entraining)	Use when freezing is a risk or to speed up setting and curing
Type IV	Only needed for massive industrial placements (special order)
Type V	Use in extreme sulfate exposure conditions

Concrete Types I, II, and III will meet most residential needs. For freeze-thaw durability, order air-entraining cement or an air-entraining admixture.

Figure 28. Effect of Adding Water to Concrete

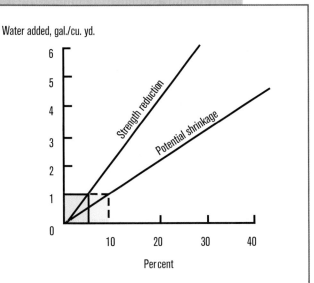

Water added, gal./cu. yd.

The more water added to a concrete mix on site, the weaker it will become, and the more it will shrink and crack. Adding 2 gallons per yard will cut compressive strength by around 10% and will increase shrinkage by close to 20%.

(**Figure 28**). On site, add the minimum amount of water needed to make the concrete workable. More water makes the concrete easier to handle, but also makes it much weaker and more prone to shrinkage and cracking (**Figure 28**).

Air Entrainment

Air entraining creates billions of microscopic air voids in hardened concrete, which serve to absorb the pressures caused by expanding ice or de-icing salts. Most ready-mix suppliers today add an air-entraining admixture to a standard cement mix.

Air entrainment is crucial for exposed concrete in cold climates, but it is

Figure 29. Concrete Slump

A slump test uses a standard cone – 12 in. high, 8 in. wide at the base, and 4 in. wide at the top. To perform the test, fill the cone in one-third lifts and "rod it" (churning by moving a piece of rebar up and down) 25 times between each lift. Remove the cone and measure the distance from the height of the cone to the height of the slumped concrete. Residential concrete should slump no more than 4 in.

recommended for almost all concrete, even in mild climates, because it reduces water demand, improves workability, reduces segregation of aggregate, and reduces bleeding of excess water. Recommended entrained-air percentages for different weather exposures are shown in **Figure 30**. Refer to the map in **Figure 31** for exposure regions throughout the continental United States.

Finishing air-entrained concrete. A concrete finisher may wait for bleed water to evaporate before starting to trowel the surface, but when concrete is air-entrained, bleed water may not appear. Excess water should still be allowed to evaporate from beneath the surface for a time before troweling begins — otherwise, water may be trapped just below a hard surface skin and cause later scaling or flaking.

Admixtures

Small amounts of specialty admixtures can be used to modify concrete properties as needed. Common admixtures are shown in **Figure 32**. More detailed information on common admixtures used in residential concrete is given below:

Figure 30. Recommended Air Entrainment for Residential Concrete

Nominal Maximum Aggregate Size (in.)	Air Content (%)*		
	Severe Exposure	Moderate Exposure	Mild Exposure
3/8	7 1/2	6	4 1/2
1/2	7	5 1/2	4
3/4	6	5	3 1/2
1	6	4 1/2	3
1 1/2	5 1/2	4 1/2	2 1/2
2	5	4	2
3	4 1/2	3 1/2	1 1/2

* Air content is specified as a percentage by volume of concrete. For severe exposure conditions, air content of the mortar alone (cement paste and sand) should be about 9%. Lower air content percentages for concrete with large aggregate reflect the fact that less mortar is needed for mixes that contain large gravel.

These levels of air-entrainment shown for different climate exposures are minimums. Higher air amounts are permissible as long as the design strength is maintained. Refer to **Figure 31** for exposure locations.

Accelerators

Accelerating admixtures are used when rapid strength gain is required, such as when the risk of freezing or tight schedules requires faster curing. Accelerators increase the heat of hydration, shorten the set time, and increase the early strength. However, they can decrease the long-term strength of the concrete. The additional heat of hydration may also contribute to increased thermal shrinkage cracking when the concrete cools.

Accelerators do not stop concrete from freezing; they only let the concrete quickly develop its air-entrainment, which gives water in concrete pores a place to go to relieve the pressure of expanding ice. When temperatures are cold, concrete may need to be protected from freezing with insulation or within a heated enclosure (see "Cold-Weather Concrete," page 39).

Calcium Chloride

Calcium chloride is one of the most common accelerators. Chlorides can increase corrosion of reinforcing steel in concrete that's exposed to de-icing salts. (Non-chloride accelerators are available but seldom specified for residential work.) Calcium chloride can be added to the truck on-site, but it is better to have the ready-mix supplier add it at the plant. Accidentally varying the dose from one truck-load to the

Figure 31. Weather Exposure Regions for Residential Concrete

- Severe
- Moderate
- Mild

"Severe" and "moderate" exposures are determined based on the likelihood that de-icing salts will be used at a given location. Check local climate data because icing conditions may vary locally with altitude.

Figure 32. Concrete Admixtures and Uses

Admixture	Common Active Ingredients	Use
Accelerator	Chloride: Calcium chloride, Non-chloride: Triethanoline (TEA), Calcium formate, Calcium nitrite	To accelerate set and strength gain (primarily used in cold weather)
Retarder	Gypsum powder, Sugar*, Lignosulfonate, Hydroxycarbolic acid	To reduce setting time (primarily used in hot weather)
Water-reducer/ plasticizer	Lignosulfonate, Hydroxycarbolic acid	To produce a more workable mix
Superplasticizer	Sulfonated melamine formaldehyde (SMF), Sulfonated naphthlene formaldehyde (SNF), Modified lignosulfate (MLS)	To produce flowing plasticizer

* Large amounts of sugar will completely stop the setting reaction, so sugar is often used as a kill when a mixer breaks down and cannot be emptied.

Admixtures are chemical or mineral compounds used to alter the physical or chemical properties of concrete.

next can cause color variations in finished slabs.

MAXIMUM DOSE = 2% CALCIUM CHLORIDE
(BY WEIGHT OF CEMENT)*

* About two 50-lb. bags of calcium chloride per 10-yd. load

Water Reducers and Plasticizers

Water reducers are used to increase slumps and make concrete more workable without adding water. This makes placement easier without compromising strength. High-range water reducers, or superplasticizers, create flowable concrete that can be readily worked into forms and around rebar, and is easily consolidated.

Superplasticizers

These can be tricky to work with. The effect from a superplasticizer typically lasts only about 30 minutes and wears off rapidly. Adding water to restore slump when the superplasticizer wears off creates inconsistent quality within the batch and should be avoided. It is possible to combine a superplasticizer with a lower-range water reducer to provide a longer working life; if you anticipate delays on site, consult with your supplier.

Set Retarders

Concrete sets up rapidly in warm weather, and it may be difficult to finish the surface before the concrete becomes too hard. Set retarders slow the rate of hydration and allow a longer working time. However, set retarders do not prevent evaporation and slump loss, so concrete may still dry out rapidly and quality can suffer. Plastic shrinkage cracking, which occurs because concrete dries out before setting, may actually be worse if a set retarder is used.

Placing Concrete

Concrete placement always happens under time pressure. Allow a half-hour to an hour per truckload of concrete — concrete is unusable after 90 minutes on the truck under normal conditions, and may go bad even faster in hot weather.

Pumping Concrete

Pumping calls for a special mix, and usually requires a specialty pumping subcontractor. Coordination is important, so a pre-construction meeting of all the contractors involved is recommended.

Pouring Concrete

Place walls in lifts of 1- to 2-ft., working around the perimeter of the building. This lets lower lifts stiffen before the pour gets deep, reducing pressure on the forms.

Place slabs in bands 4- to 6-ft.-wide, and strike off as you go so you won't have to disturb concrete that has already begun to set.

Place concrete close to its final position. Don't puddle it in one place and drag it along — the farther the concrete is pulled, the more the gravel separates from the paste (segregates), causing honeycombing and weakening the structure.

Do not drop the concrete more than 4 ft. Use a drop-chute with a 6-in.-diameter rubber or canvas hose to prevent segregation of aggregate.

Compact concrete as you place it by rodding, spading, or vibrating. This removes large air bubbles and prevents voids.

Finishing Concrete

Strike off and bullfloat concrete as soon as it is placed, but wait for bleed water to evaporate before starting to trowel. Working concrete with water on the surface creates a weak layer and leads to dusting, crazing, and scaling. If concrete starts to set up before bleed water evaporates, sweep the bleed water off with a rubber hose or squeegee.

Edging is required to compact concrete near forms. Wait until bleed water evaporates to begin edging, but right after bullfloating, slip a mason's trowel down between the form and the concrete to cut the two apart in preparation for edging later.

Jointing. Joints can be made in the slab while it's still soft. The grooving tool must cut through the slab one-quarter its thickness to make the joint an effective control against shrinkage cracking (see "Control Joints," page 65).

Floating drives aggregate just below the surface and removes surface imperfections. Floating should be done after edging and jointing, but before final troweling.

Troweling. Concrete is ready for hand-troweling when the weight of a worker makes a 1/4-in. heel-mark on the slab. For machine troweling (power-troweling), the concrete should be harder — a heel mark should be only 1/8-in.-deep.

Stripping forms. Allow concrete in forms to reach at least 500 psi compressive strength before stripping forms. This typically takes a day in mild weather, or three days in cold weather. Concrete suppliers can provide maturity curves that estimate the strength development of specific concrete mixes under specific field conditions — when in doubt, rely on the supplier's data.

Curing Concrete

Concrete hardens not by drying, but by hydration — a chemical reaction between cement and water. This reaction needs moisture and warmth. Curing is the technique of keeping the concrete moist and at the correct temperature (50°F to 90°F) for a period of at least three to seven days (the shorter period applies to concrete made with high-early-strength cement or with an accelerating admixture). If cured properly, concrete will be stronger, more abrasion-resistant, more durable, and less permeable.

Curing Problems

Drying out. If concrete dries out before curing is complete, hydration stops. Hardening will resume if the concrete becomes wet again, but in the

Figure 33. Slab Curing Techniques

Method	Advantages	Disadvantages	Comments
Cover with plastic sheeting	Low cost, easy to handle, effective, does not leave film on slab	May mottle slab surface; can be torn or disturbed	Use large pieces to minimize joints, seal carefully, inspect and maintain, save for reuse
Apply spray curing compound	Cheap, simple, does not require maintenance or monitoring	Coverage may be incomplete if not applied with care; film may prevent bonding of finish floor; may not work in cold weather	Select opaque disappearing brand to monitor coverage; consult with suppliers concerning floor bonding
Continuous sprinkling or cover with wet burlap	Highly effective if sprinkled continuously, or burlap kept wet is used	Requires monitoring; may create runoff	Use clean water, provide drainage, monitor and maintain
Ponding	Best results if maintained continuously for prescribed period	Complicated; requires maintenance and monitoring; may cause runoff	May be practical for enclosed slabs (basements) and small areas

Special attention must be given to curing concrete slabs because their relatively large surface area gives up moisture and heat quickly. Proper curing keeps the moisture and temperature in the concrete as long as possible.

field it is hard to resaturate concrete, so maintaining moisture for the minimum time is a better course.

Freezing. Concrete that freezes before reaching compressive strength of 500 psi may be ruined. If it freezes after reaching 500 psi, however, it will continue to harden when it warms up, as long as sufficient water is present. Again, maintaining good curing conditions for a few days is better than trying to reestablish them later.

Curing Conditions

Concrete is "comfortable" if people are comfortable. The best time to pour concrete work is when the weather is between 50°F and 70°F, humid, and not too sunny. In these conditions, little extra effort is required to cure concrete.

For walls in normal weather, leaving the forms in place will keep water trapped in the wall and allow curing to continue. The wall top should be kept wet with a soaker hose, or sealed with a spray-applied curing compound. If forms have to be stripped, spray the whole wall with curing compound or cover it with plastic sheeting (seal all seams and penetrations).

For slabs during mild weather, practical curing methods include ponding, sprinkling continuously, covering with plastic, covering with wet burlap, or sealing with a spray-applied curing compound. Each method has advantages and disadvantages (**Figure 33**). Spraying on a curing compound has become the most popular method because the one-time step is quick, simple, and cheap; but the coatings may prevent the adhesion of tile or other floor coverings, and care must be taken to get full coverage.

Weather Conditions

Extreme weather presents challenges for placing, handling, and curing concrete. By slowing down hydration, cold weather delays setting times and slows strength gain; plus, concrete may be damaged or ruined by freezing. Hot weather speeds up hydration and causes rapid drying, which can lead to various finish defects and structural weakness. Slabs are especially vulnerable to either cold or heat; if possible, slab work should be rescheduled for better weather.

Cold-Weather Concrete

With concrete, cold weather refers to temperatures averaging lower than 40°F, or dropping below 50°F for more than half the day.

When placing concrete in cold weather, take these precautions:

- **Thaw forms and subgrade.** Never place concrete on frozen ground or in icy or frosty forms. Ice and frost-swelled soil can fill the space meant to contain concrete, leaving future voids. Concrete may freeze instead of hardening, and could be damaged or weakened. Frost heave of soil after concrete is placed also may damage footings, walls, or slabs.

Figure 34. Cold-Weather Guidelines for Concrete Walls and Footings

TYPE I CEMENT

Predicted low temperature prior to concrete reaching 500-psi compressive strength:

32°F to 20°F
Min. 470 lb. cement/yd. (5-sack mix)
Temperature of concrete: Min. of 60°F
Max. 6-in. slump
1% Calcium Chloride or equivalent accelerator
No protection required

19°F to 10°F
Min. 517 lb. cement/yd. (51/2-sack mix)
Temperature of concrete: Min. of 60°F
Max. 6-in. slump
2% Calcium Chloride or equivalent accelerator
No protection required

9°F to 0°F
Min. 564-lb. cement/yd. (6-sack mix)
Temperature of concrete: Min. of 60°F
Max. 6-in. slump
2% Calcium Chloride or equivalent accelerator
Cover top of wall with 6-ft.-wide insulated blanket

Below 0°F
Min. 564 lb. cement/yd. (6-sack mix)
Temperature of concrete: Min. of 60°F
Max. 6-in. slump
2% Calcium Chloride or equivalent accelerator
Cover entire wall with an insulated blanket or cover and provide auxiliary heat

TYPE III CEMENT

Predicted low temperature prior to concrete reaching 500-psi compressive strength:

32°F to 20°F
Min. 470 lb. cement/yd. (5-sack mix)
Temperature of concrete: Min. of 60°F
Max. 6-in. slump
No accelerator
No protection required

19°F to 10°F
Min. 517 lb. cement/yd. (51/2-sack mix)
Temperature of concrete: Min. of 60°F
Max. 6-in. slump
1% Calcium Chloride or equivalent accelerator

9°F to 0°F
Min. 564 lb. cement/yd. (6-sack mix)
Temperature of concrete: Min. of 60°F
Max. 6-in. slump
2% Calcium Chloride or equivalent accelerator
No protection required

Below 0°F
Min. 564 lb. cement/yd. (6-sack mix)
Temperature of concrete: Min. of 60°F
Max. 6-in. slump
2% Calcium Chloride or equivalent accelerator
Cover top of wall with 6-ft.-wide insulated blanket

For each type of cement used, follow these mix and protection guidelines to prevent freezing of plain, unreinforced concrete. Note: These recommendations are designed to prevent freezing damage to green concrete, but may not provide ideal curing conditions.

To thaw ground and forms, cover them with straw or blankets, or build a heated enclosure. Make sure exhaust from heaters goes outside the enclosure; otherwise workers may be poisoned from carbon monoxide. Carbon dioxide in exhaust can also damage concrete surfaces.

- **Adjust mix for rapid strength gain.** Follow the supplier's recommendations for an appropriate mix for the placement and end-use weather conditions. To generate extra heat and speed up strength gain, options include adding extra cement to the mix, using Type III cement, or using an accelerating admixture (in very cold weather, all three strategies may be combined). General recommendations for cold-weather mixes and curing protection are shown in **Figure 34**.

- **Check concrete temperature.** Concrete coming down the chute should be at 60°F. Make your supplier aware of your expectations and be ready to reject loads that are cooler than 55°F.

- **Protect subgrade from freezing before and after pour.** Even after concrete is cured, frost heaves in soil can crack structures. To prevent this, insulate slabs, footings, and walls; cap foundation quickly; backfill as soon as possible; and heat structure.

Figure 35. Concrete Temperature vs. Set Time

Concrete Temperature (F°)	Set Time (hrs.)
70	6
60	8
50	11
40	14
30	19

Cold-Weather Finishing

In cold weather, set times are delayed (**Figure 35**) so schedule the pour early in the day. In cold temperatures (below 40°F), don't be surprised if finishing has to be done at night, long after regular quitting time. Bleed water may not evaporate; be ready to squeegee it off the slab. Slabs cool rapidly, so be ready to protect the slab with insulating blankets and straw as soon as finish troweling is complete.

Cold-Weather Curing

Ponding and sprinkling are impractical in freezing weather. Use curing compounds or plastic sheeting to hold moisture in fresh concrete. Provide enough insulation to keep concrete temperature above 50°F for at least three days (seven days is preferable). See **Figure 36** for the insulation level needed to maintain adequate warmth and **Figure 37** for insulation materials to meet R-value requirements.

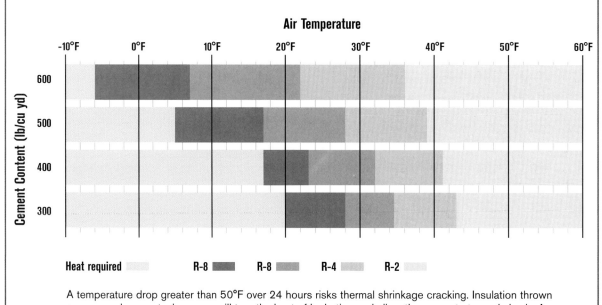

Figure 36. Insulation Required to Keep Concrete at 55°F

A temperature drop greater than 50°F over 24 hours risks thermal shrinkage cracking. Insulation thrown over poured concrete, however, will trap the heat of hydration and allow the concrete to cool slowly. As outside air temperature drops, it may become harder to keep concrete at the correct temperature using insulation alone. Below a certain point for any given mix, provide a heated enclosure to prevent damage to the concrete from freezing.

Figure 37. R-Values of Common Material

Material	R-Value
1/2-in. plywood	0.5
1-in. straw	2.0
1-in. mineral fiber blanket	3.0
1-in. expanded polyurethane	6.0

After curing, exposed slabs need to dry thoroughly before they can withstand winter freezing. For that reason, pouring slabs in late fall is risky in colder regions.

Hot-Weather Concrete

Rapid evaporation causes most of the hot-weather problems for concrete. If sweat is evaporating quickly off workers, chances are that moisture is evaporating quickly from the concrete as well. Take these precautions:

- **Wet forms and subgrade.** Use a spray hose or sprinkler to dampen work area before beginning. Soak area well, but do not create standing water. Soaking the subgrade the night before the pour may be most practical.

- **Chill the mix.** You can order concrete made with chilled water or even shaved ice. Some suppliers can refrigerate their aggregate also. Concrete should not be hotter than 60°F coming off the truck.

- **Provide shade and wind protection.** Sun screens, movable awnings, and wind barriers can reduce evaporation rates.

- **Fog the work.** Rent a fogging sprayer to elevate the humidity around the slab.

- **Retemper with care.** It's okay to replace water lost to evaporation, but not to add water to a partially hydrated load. In practice, add no more than a gallon or two per yard. Add this at the beginning, not midway through the load.

- **Adjust schedule.** Start work at sunup and finish before noon, or work in late evening.

- **Adjust manpower.** Have extra help ready to place and finish concrete quickly. If your normal crew is four people, add a fifth or sixth person.

- **Schedule work in stages.** Don't pour too far ahead of yourself — place small sections of slab that you can finish with the available labor.

Hot-Weather Finishing

Start to trowel as soon as bleed water has evaporated. Do not trowel water back into slab or sprinkle water onto slab (this causes crazing and flaking). However, if concrete begins to harden before water has evaporated, drag the water off with a hose or squeegee.

Hot-Weather Curing

For walls, apply curing compound to wall top right away, and to wall sides as soon as forms are stripped, or cover completely with plastic. Seal all plastic seams and penetrations, and ensure complete coverage with curing compound.

For slabs, start curing (cover with plastic or ponded water, spray on curing compound, or begin sprinkling) as soon as troweling is complete. Concrete must not be allowed to dry out.

Do not cover with black plastic, which absorbs solar heat and can cause too-rapid hydration or drying. Clear plastic is better, and reflective white plastic is best.

Footings

Footings serve to spread the load onto the soil for adequate bearing, and to provide a smooth, level surface for wall forms or for block and mortar work. Footings also resist lateral soil pressure at the base of foundation walls.

Footing Layout

Footings can be larger than required dimensions, but should not be smaller. Footings should be straight and level to within 1/4 in. over 20 ft., and should be no more than 1/2-in. out of square in 20 ft.

Figure 38. Minimum Width of Concrete or Masonry Footings (in.)

	Loadbearing Value of Soil (psf)					
	1,500	**2,000**	**2,500**	**3,000**	**3,500**	**4,000**
Conventional Wood Frame Construction						
1-story	16in.	12in.	10in.	8in.	7in.	6in.
2-story	19	15	12	10	8	7
3-story	22	17	14	11	10	9
4-in. Brick Veneer over Wood Frame or 8-in. Hollow Concrete Masonry						
1-story	19 in.	15 in.	12 in.	10 in.	8 in.	7 in.
2-story	25	19	15	13	11	10
3-story	31	23	19	16	13	12
8-in. Solid or Fully Grouted Masonry						
1-story	22 in.	17 in.	13 in.	11 in.	10 in.	9 in.
2-story	31	23	19	16	13	12
3-story	40	30	24	20	17	15

The width of a foundation footing is based on the loadbearing value of the soil. Load-values assume undisturbed, native soils of known type or tested values of compacted soils.

2000 International Residential Code

Footing Width

The bearing width of footings varies according to soil strengths and loading conditions (**Figure 38**).

Footing Tie-In

Footings should be struck off level, but should never be troweled smooth. In addition, footings must be tied firmly to the wall above using either a keyway poured into the footing or reinforcing bar projecting from the footing into the concrete (**Figure 39**).

Footing Thickness

Footing proportions for plain concrete (unreinforced) footings are set by code (**Figure 40**, left and center). Generally, footings should be at least as deep as the thickness of the wall they support. The wall should be centered on the footing so that the projection of the footing on each side equals half the wall or footing thickness.

If a wider footing is required, the footing must be reinforced (**Figure 40**, right). Typically, 1/2-in. or 5/8-in. rebar will be required on 1-ft. centers, set about 3 in. up from the bottom of the footing.

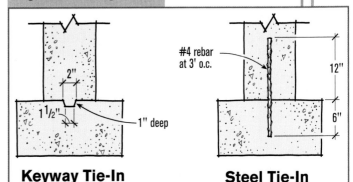

Figure 39. Footing Tie-In

#4 rebar at 3' o.c.

2"

1 1/2"

1" deep

12"

6"

Keyway Tie-In   **Steel Tie-In**

Concrete requires a subbase of compacted stone fill. The subbase adds support and serves as a capillary break for preventing frost heaves from cracking the brittle surface.

Frost Depth

The footing should be placed at least 1 ft. below the frost line so it will not heave when the soil freezes. Frost depth varies depending on local climate; check with local codes for the local frost depth. On a hillside foundation (such as a basement walkout), plan on building a frostwall on the downslope side (**Figure 41**).

As an alternative to building a frost-wall, a walk-out basement may be insulated to protect against frost damage (see "Insulation for Walkout Basements," page 115).

Shallow foundations may offer an alternative to deep excavations if properly insulated and detailed. See "Frost-Protected Shallow Foundations," page 113.

Figure 40. Footing Dimensions

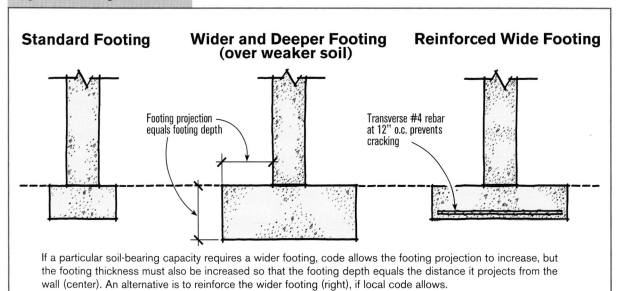

Standard Footing

Wider and Deeper Footing
(over weaker soil)

Reinforced Wide Footing

Footing projection
equals footing depth

Transverse #4 rebar
at 12" o.c. prevents
cracking

If a particular soil-bearing capacity requires a wider footing, code allows the footing projection to increase, but the footing thickness must also be increased so that the footing depth equals the distance it projects from the wall (center). An alternative is to reinforce the wider footing (right), if local code allows.

Figure 41. Frostwall for Basement Walkout

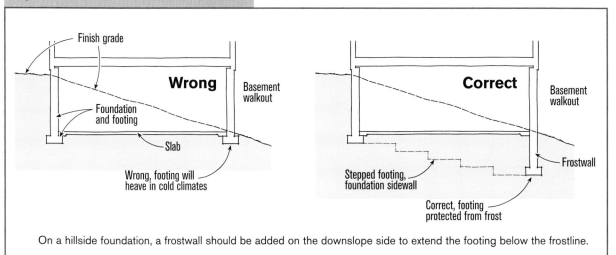

Finish grade

Wrong

Basement
walkout

Foundation
and footing

Slab

Wrong, footing will
heave in cold climates

Correct

Basement
walkout

Frostwall

Stepped footing,
foundation sidewall

Correct, footing
protected from frost

On a hillside foundation, a frostwall should be added on the downslope side to extend the footing below the frostline.

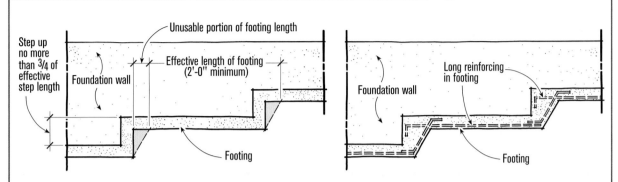

Figure 42. Stepped Footings

The rise of a stepped footing should not exceed 2 ft., and the footing should run at least 2 ft. horizontally between steps (left). Typically, the corners of a stepped excavation are unstable. The footing should be sloped and reinforced, so the effective horizontal length of the footing is supported on well-compacted soil (right).

Stepped Footings

On sloped sites, footings must be kept level, so the footings will have to be stepped. Step lengths must be at least 2 ft., step heights must be no greater than three-quarters of step length, and vertical footing sections must be at least 6 in. thick (**Figure 42**).

On slopes too steep for stepped footings of these dimensions, consider a pier-and-grade-beam foundation (see "Pier Foundations," page 97).

Figure 43. Jump Footings

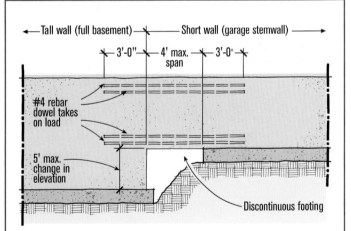

For poured concrete wall only: Where a garage steamwall abuts a main basement wall, the short section of wall can be reinforced to span the gap. Use two #4 bars at the top and bottom of the short wall, extending 3 ft. into each adjoining section of wall above the footings. This solution is limited to a 4-ft. maximum span and a 5-ft. maximum change in elevation. If the walls are at right angles, the rebar can be bent accordingly.

Figure 44. Pouring Footings in a Wet Trench

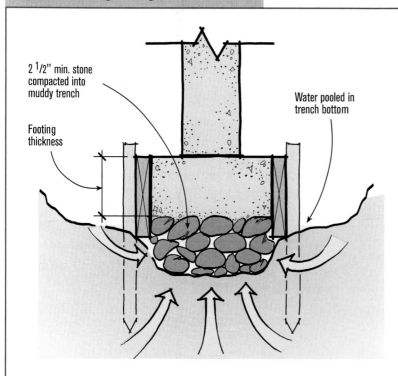

2 1/2" min. stone compacted into muddy trench

Footing thickness

Water pooled in trench bottom

When water pools in a footing trench, place large cobbles in the bottom of the form, compacting them down into the mud. Muck and water may fill the places between the stones, but contact between stones will provide bearing. Use a stiff concrete mix when casting the footings.

Jump Footings

When a short foundation wall ties into a tall wall (such as where a house with a full basement jumps to a stem wall for the garage), the footing can be interrupted and the foundation wall tied together with a reinforced foundation wall section. Masonry foundation walls have no real spanning capability, so the footing must be stepped down when elevations change, but poured concrete walls can be reinforced with steel to span openings (**Figure 43**, previous page). Check with a local code official first; the code on the books may have been written for masonry foundations.

Footing Problems

Foundation walls should be centered on the footing. In the event of a layout mistake, the footing can be repaired. The repair depends on the soil conditions.

A well-compacted gravel support may be allowed, but usually must be based on a good soil analysis and an engineer's approval. Otherwise, an augmented footing must be poured using rebar dowels epoxied into the existing footing (**Figure 45**).

When footing trenches fill up with water in wet conditions, place a layer of well-tamped 3- to 4-in. cobbles (**Figure 44**) and use a stiff concrete mix when casting the footings.

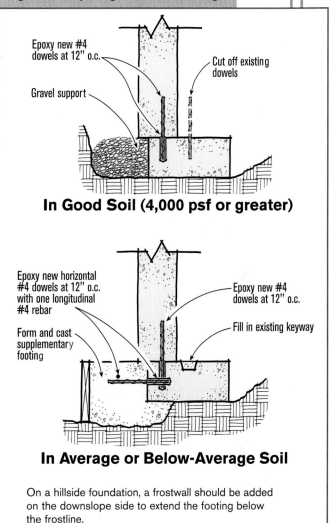

Figure 45. Repairing Off-Center Footings

Epoxy new #4 dowels at 12" o.c.

Gravel support

Cut off existing dowels

In Good Soil (4,000 psf or greater)

Epoxy new horizontal #4 dowels at 12" o.c. with one longitudinal #4 rebar

Form and cast supplementary footing

Epoxy new #4 dowels at 12" o.c.

Fill in existing keyway

In Average or Below-Average Soil

On a hillside foundation, a frostwall should be added on the downslope side to extend the footing below the frostline.

Rebar

Figure 46. Rebar for Poured Foundation Walls

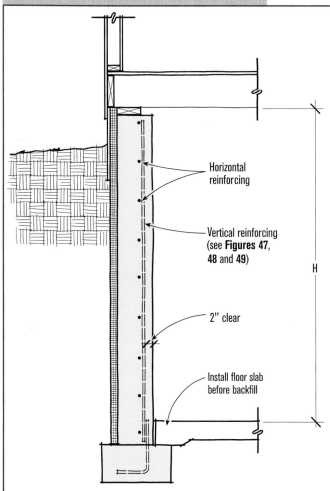

Horizontal reinforcing

Vertical reinforcing (see **Figures 47, 48** and **49**)

H

2" clear

Install floor slab before backfill

Place rebar towards the tension side of a concrete foundation wall that is pinned in place by floor framing and a basement slab. If the concrete wall is thicker than 10 in., a second layer of reinforcing, placed near the outside face, is recommended.

How Rebar Works

When a sideways load is applied to a concrete wall, *tension* develops on the pressure-bearing side and *compression* develops on the side away from the load. In a free-standing retaining wall, the tension side is on the earth side of the wall (**Figure 73**, page 82). In a foundation wall that is held in place by floor framing and a basement slab, the tension side is on the inside (**Figure 46**, and **Figure 66**, page 75). Concrete resists the compression, while the steel carries the tension and prevents the structure from breaking and toppling.

> **Caution**
> Exposed rebar is dangerous. Cover exposed ends with rubber caps.

Figure 47. Foundation Wall Reinforcements for Well-Drained Sites (8-in. wall thickness)

Maximum Wall Height (ft.)	Maximum Unbalanced Backfill Height[5] (ft.)	GM, GC, SM, GW, GP, SW and SP soils	SM-SC and ML soils	SC, MH, ML-CL and inorganic CL soils
6	5	#4 at 48" o.c.	#4 at 48" o.c.	#4 at 48" o.c.
	6	#4 at 48" o.c.	#4 at 40" o.c.	#5 at 48" o.c.
7	4	#4 at 48" o.c.	#4 at 48" o.c.	#4 at 48" o.c.
	5	#4 at 48" o.c.	#4 at 48" o.c.	#4 at 40" o.c.
	6	#4 at 48" o.c.	#5 at 48" o.c.	#5 at 40" o.c.
	7	#4 at 40" o.c.	#5 at 40" o.c.	#6 at 48" o.c.
8	5	#4 at 48" o.c.	#4 at 48" o.c.	#4 at 40" o.c.
	6	#4 at 48" o.c.	#5 at 48" o.c.	#5 at 40" o.c.
	7	#5 at 48" o.c.	#6 at 48" o.c.	#6 at 40" o.c.
	8	#5 at 40" o.c.	#6 at 40" o.c.	#6 at 24" o.c.
9	5	#4 at 48" o.c.	#4 at 48" o.c.	#5 at 48" o.c.
	6	#4 at 48" o.c.	#5 at 48" o.c.	#6 at 48" o.c.
	7	#5 at 48" o.c.	#6 at 48" o.c.	#6 at 32" o.c.
	8	#5 at 40" o.c.	#6 at 32" o.c.	#6 at 24" o.c.
	9	#6 at 40" o.c.	#6 at 24" o.c.	#6 at 16" o.c.

Header: Minimum Vertical Reinforcement Size and Spacing[1], [2] for 8-in. Nominal Wall Thickness[3] — Soil Classes[4]

(1) Alternative reinforcing bar sizes and spacings having an equivalent cross-sectional area of reinforcement per lineal foot of wall are permitted by code, provided the spacing of the reinforcement does not exceed 72 in.

(2) Use minimum Grade 60 rebar. The distance from the face of the soil side of the wall to the center of vertical reinforcement must be at least 5 in.

(3) For masonry walls, use Type M or S mortar and lay masonry in a running bond. See "Concrete Block Foundations," page 67.

(4) Soil classes refer to symbols explained in **Figure 5,** page 4.

(5) Unbalanced backfill height is the difference in height of the exterior and interior finish ground levels. Where an interior concrete slab is provided, the unbalanced backfill height is measured from the exterior finish ground level to the top of the interior concrete slab.

The allowable designs shown here apply only to block and poured concrete foundations that sit above the seasonal water table and are not located in a seismic zone (see **Figures 48** and **49** for reinforcing schedules to meet these other site conditions).

Adapted from 2000 International Residential Code

Figure 48. Foundation Wall Reinforcement for Seismic Zones (12-in. wall thickness)

Maximum Wall Height (ft.)	Maximum Unbalanced Backfill Height[5] (ft.)	Vertical Reinforcement Size and Spacing[1], [2] for 12-in. Nominal Wall Thickness[3]		
		Soil Classes[4]		
		GW, GP, SW and SP soils	GM, GC, SM, SM-SC and ML soils	SC, MH, ML-CL and inorganic CL soils
7	4	#4 at 72" o.c.	#4 at 72" o.c.	#4 at 72" o.c.
	5	#4 at 72" o.c.	#4 at 72" o.c.	#4 at 72" o.c.
	6	#4 at 72" o.c.	#4 at 64" o.c.	#4 at 48" o.c.
	7	#4 at 72" o.c.	#4 at 48" o.c.	#5 at 56" o.c.
8	4	#4 at 72" o.c.	#4 at 72" o.c.	#4 at 72" o.c.
	5	#4 at 72" o.c.	#4 at 56" o.c.	#5 at 72" o.c.
	6	#4 at 64" o.c.	#5 at 64" o.c.	#4 at 32" o.c.
	7	#4 at 48" o.c.	#4 at 32" o.c.	#5 at 40" o.c.
9	5	#4 at 72" o.c.	#4 at 72" o.c.	#4 at 72" o.c.
	6	#4 at 72" o.c.	#4 at 56" o.c.	#5 at 64" o.c.
	7	#4 at 56" o.c.	#4 at 40" o.c.	#6 at 64" o.c.
	8	#4 at 64" o.c.	#6 at 64" o.c.	#6 at 48" o.c.
	9	#5 at 56" o.c.	#7 at 72" o.c.	#6 at 40" o.c.

(1) Alternative reinforcing bar sizes and spacings having an equivalent cross-sectional area of reinforcement per lineal foot of wall are permitted by code, provided the spacing of the reinforcement does not exceed 72 in.

(2) Use minimum Grade 60 rebar. The distance from the face of the soil side of the wall to the center of vertical reinforcement must be at least 8.75 in.

(3) For masonry walls, use Type M or S mortar and lay masonry in a running bond. See "Concrete Block Foundations," page 67.

(4) Soil classes refer to symbols explained in **Figure 5**, page 4.

(5) Unbalanced backfill height is the difference in height of the exterior and interior finish ground levels. Where an interior concrete slab is provided, the unbalanced backfill height is measured from the exterior finish ground level to the top of the interior concrete slab.

Adapted from 2000 International Residential Code

Rebar Sizes

Rebar comes in a range of diameters, numbered 3 through 11. The numbers denote the diameter of the bar in $1/8$-in. increments. Thus, #3 bar is $3/8$ in. in diameter, #4 bar is $4/8$ (or $1/2$) in., #5 bar is $5/8$ in., and so on. The size most commonly used in residential construction is #4, though #5 and #6 bar are used often in hillside construction and tall concrete walls in seismic zones. Walkways, pool decks, steps, and simple landings often use #3 bar.

Rebar Grades

Rebar is graded in primary classifications, commonly known as grade 40 and grade 60. Grade 40 is more malleable and easier to bend. Grade 60 is stiffer and does not bend as easily. Typically, Grade 40 is found in #3 and #4 bar, and Grade 60 in #5 and larger.

Size and Spacing In Walls

Figure 47 shows proper reinforcement size and spacing for standard 8-in.-thick concrete and masonry walls at various heights. "Standard" construction implies work on well-drained sites with stable soils and the use of granular backfills and perimeter drains.

Reinforcement for Seismic Forces

In seismic zones, code requires extra reinforcement. For foundations supporting more than 4 ft. of unbalanced fill, follow the schedules shown in **Figure 48** and **Figure 49**. For best results, err on the side of placing more rebar, and always backfill the foundation with a free-draining granular soil to reduce lateral forces (see "Backfill," page 109).

Reinforcement for Wet Sites

On sites with high seasonal water tables that will exert increased hydrostatic pressure on foundations, all codes require engineering.

Figure 49. Foundation Wall Thickness for Seismic Zones (10-in. wall thickness)

Maximum Wall Height (ft.)	Maximum Unbalanced Backfill Height[5] (ft.)	Minimum Vertical Reinforcement Size and Spacing[1], [2] for 8-in. Nominal Wall Thickness[3] Soil Classes[4]		
		GM, GC, SM, GW, GP, SW and SP soils	SM-SC and ML soils	SC, MH, ML-CL and inorganic CL soils
7	4	#4 at 56" o.c.	#4 at 56" o.c.	#4 at 56" o.c.
	5	#4 at 56" o.c.	#4 at 56" o.c.	#4 at 56" o.c.
	6	#4 at 56" o.c.	#4 at 48" o.c.	#4 at 40" o.c.
	7	#4 at 56" o.c.	#5 at 56" o.c.	#5 at 40" o.c.
8	5	#4 at 56" o.c.	#4 at 56" o.c.	#4 at 48" o.c.
	6	#4 at 56" o.c.	#4 at 48" o.c.	#5 at 56" o.c.
	7	#4 at 48" o.c.	#4 at 32" o.c.	#6 at 56" o.c.
	8	#5 at 56" o.c.	#5 at 40" o.c.	#7 at 56" o.c.
9	5	#4 at 56" o.c.	#4 at 56" o.c.	#4 at 48" o.c.
	6	#4 at 56" o.c.	#4 at 40" o.c.	#4 at 32" o.c.
	7	#4 at 56" o.c.	#5 at 48" o.c.	#6 at 48" o.c.
	8	#4 at 32" o.c.	#6 at 48" o.c.	#4 at 16" o.c.
	9	#5 at 40" o.c.	#6 at 40" o.c.	#7 at 40" o.c.

(1) Alternative reinforcing bar sizes and spacings having an equivalent cross-sectional area of reinforcement per lineal foot of wall are permitted by code, provided the spacing of the reinforcement does not exceed 72 in.

(2) Use minimum Grade 60 rebar. The distance from the face of the soil side of the wall to the center of vertical reinforcement must be at least 6.75 in.

(3) For masonry walls, use Type M or S mortar and lay masonry in a running bond. See "Concrete Block Foundations," page 67.

(4) Soil classes refer to symbols explained in **Figure 5**, page 4.

(5) Unbalanced backfill height is the difference in height of the exterior and interior finish ground levels. Where an interior concrete slab is provided, the unbalanced backfill height is measured from the exterior finish ground level to the top of the interior concrete slab.

Adapted from 2000 International Residential Code

Placing Rebar In Walls

Rebar should always be placed near the **tension side** of the concrete.

In a full-height foundation wall, which is held in place by floor framing at the top and by the footing at the bottom, the tension side is toward the inside (**Figure 46**, and **Figure 66**, page 75).

In a free-standing retaining wall or a half-height foundation wall, the tension would be on the side nearest the ground load (see "Stepped Foundation Walls," page 64).

Horizontal rebar is most effective along the top and bottom of the foundation elevation.

Concrete Coverage Over Rebar

To prevent corrosion, rebar must be covered with concrete:

- In pads and footings: 3-in. minimum coverage.

- In walls and slabs #6 or larger requires 2-in. minimum coverage; #5 or smaller needs $1^1/_2$-in. minimum coverage.

Splicing Rebar

Tie all rebar with wire at splices. Overlap splices by 24 bar diameters (12-in. overlap for #4 bar, 15-in. overlap for #5 bar, 18-in. overlap for #6 bar), or as specified by an engineer.

Anchors

Code Requirements

By code, all exterior sill plates must be anchored with minimum 1/2-in.-diameter anchor bolts.

Spacing

When casting foundations, place anchors at a maximum of 6 ft. o.c., and within 12 in. from the ends of each plate section.

Embedment Depth

Foundation anchors must extend a minimum of 7 in. into concrete.

Placing Anchor Bolts

Where anchor posts attach to a corner stud or at one side of a wall opening, they must be located precisely. A layout jig can be very helpful (**Figure 50**). If possible, wire the anchor posts directly to the rebar.

Seismic Anchors

In seismic zones, all shear walls must be mechanically fastened to the foundation with metal hold-downs, metal straps, closed-space anchor bolts, or some combination of these (**Figure 51**). Hold-downs require anchor bolts

Figure 50. Anchor Bolt Layout Jig

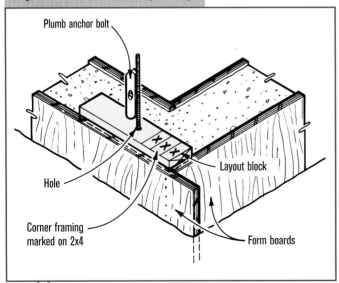

Plumb anchor bolt

Layout block

Hole

Corner framing
marked on 2x4

Form boards

Figure 51. Seismic Anchor Types

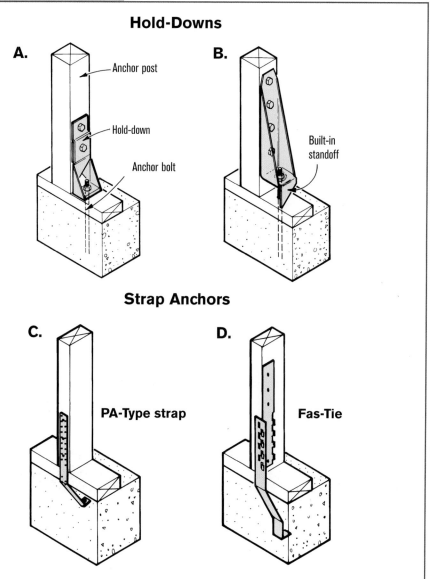

Hold-Downs

A.

Anchor post

Hold-down

Anchor bolt

B.

Built-in
standoff

Strap Anchors

C.

PA-Type strap

D.

Fas-Tie

Hold-downs either sit directly on the sill or bottom plate (**A**), or have a built-in standoff
that lifts them off the plate (**B**) so the bolt-holes won't split out the end of the post.
Strap anchors nail either directly to the stud (**C**), or through the sheathing into the stud.
A two-part anchor (**D**) has two parts that lock together – one piece embedded in the
concrete and a second piece nailed to the wide face of the stud.

Figure 52. Hold-Down Anchor Bolts

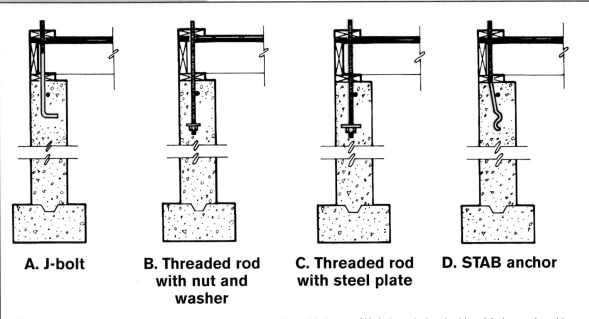

A. J-bolt **B. Threaded rod with nut and washer** **C. Threaded rod with steel plate** **D. STAB anchor**

There are four types of anchor bolts for use with foundation hold-downs: (A) A threaded rod with a 90-degree bend in the end, like a large J-bolt; (B) a threaded rod or long bolt with a nut and washer on the end; (C) a threaded rod with a 1/4-in.-thick steel plate bolted to the end; and (D) a manufactured anchor bolt, such as Simpson Strong-Tie's STAB anchor.

that extend up though the floor framing (**Figure 52**).

Code Requirements in Seismic Zones

In addition to following the anchor spacing requirements described above, code specifies:

- A minimum anchor spacing of 4 ft. o.c. for two-story buildings
- Anchors located within 12 in. of the ends of each plate section for all interior bearing walls and interior braced wall lines, as well as all exterior walls
- Plate washers measuring at least 2x2x^3/16 in.

Retrofit Foundation Anchors

A variety of foundation anchors can be used to retrofit a missing anchor bolt

Selecting and Placing Concrete Anchors

Sill plate for bearing wall. If you've left out one or two anchor bolts, a few powder-actuated fasteners (PAFs) should do the job. If the slab is uneven and you need to draw the plate down, use a sleeve anchor. If you've left out all the anchor bolts for a bearing wall, use sleeve, wedge, or epoxy anchors.

Sole plate to slab for nonloadbearing partition. A PAF is the fastest way to connect interior partition plates (wood or steel) to a slab. Hammer anchors are a good alternative.

Steel column to a slab. To secure the bearing plate of a structural post to a concrete slab, use a wedge or epoxy anchor. If the concrete is at all soft, an epoxy anchor is more reliable.

Ledger for exterior deck or porch. To attach a framing ledger to a poured concrete or masonry wall, use a wedge anchor for strength. You may want to use a PAF to hold the ledger level while you're drilling for the wedge anchors.

Stair stringer in concrete bulkhead. A PAF is sufficient if you can fasten every 16 in. or so along the stringer. If you have to hang the stairs from one end of the stairwell, you're better off depending on a sleeve or wedge anchor.

Sleepers for wood flooring over a slab. A PAF will work well, unless the slab is way out of level (if it slopes towards a drain, for example). In this case, with shims beneath the sleepers, you may exceed the length of a PAF and need to use a wedge or sleeve anchor in the deepest areas.

Wood frame around basement openings. To box out a door or window with pressure-treated wood, PAFs are the quickest option; concrete screws or hammer anchors will also work.

Strapping to foundation wall. When fastening nailers for drywall or siding to a poured concrete or masonry wall, PAFs are the fastest method. Drive the pin into the horizontal mortar joint of a masonry wall. Concrete screws or hammer anchors are an alternative.

or fasten framing into foundation materials (**Figure 53**). While many of these anchors are more expensive than shields or drop-in anchors, they don't require laborious spotting, which is difficult and time-consuming.

Selecting Retrofit Anchors

Follow the guidelines shown in **Figure 53** when retrofitting concrete anchors.

Figure 53. Typical Retrofit Concrete Anchors

Anchor Type	Size (in.)	Minimum Embedment Depth (in.)	Pullout Strength (lbs.) (3,000-psi concrete except as noted)
Hammer (sleeve type)	$1/4$ x 2	$3/4$	800
Hammer (nail type)	$1/4$ x $2^1/4$	$1^1/4$	1,100
PAF	.140 x $2^1/2$	$1^1/4$	1,400
Concrete screw	$1/4$ x $2^3/4$	$1^1/2$	1,500
Sleeve	$3/8$ x 3	$1^5/8$	2,400
Wedge	$3/8$ x 4	3	4,000–5,000 (4,000-psi concrete)
Epoxy (dispenser type)	$3/8$ x 4	$3^1/2$	5,000–7,000 (4,000-psi concrete)
Epoxy (capsule type)	$3/8$ x 4	$3^1/2$	5,000–7,000 (4,000-psi concrete)

The sizes shown are typical for the type of fastener, although other sizes are available. Valves are typical only for the size listed and should be checked for the specific fastener and substrate. Values listed are "ultimate" pullout strength. In actual design, a safety factor of 4:1 to 8:1 is typically used.

Tips for Placing Concrete Anchors

Usually the most important detail in installing any type of mechanical or epoxy anchor is drilling the hole according to the manufacturer's specs.

Do not drill too close to a concrete or masonry edge, or the anchor is likely to break out the substrate when inserted, and holding power may be compromised.

If the diameter of the hole is too large, concrete screws won't tap and hold properly, while sleeve and wedge anchors may spin in the hole.

Concrete screws will require a hole $1/4$ in. deeper than the screw to leave room for displaced material, and drop-in anchors may fail if not placed in holes drilled to a required depth.

Overtightening may compromise the holding power of sleeve and wedge anchors. Take care to torque them down to manufacturer's specifications. Some anchors are also sensitive to the depth of the hole.

Retrofit Anchors in Unstable Substrates

For best results, place anchors in stable concrete. If you are uncertain if the concrete or masonry is stable, choose an epoxy anchor, which will help bind the base material together. Check with the manufacturer or catalog for the appropriate embedment depth and design load of each fastener —especially for any structural connections.

Poured Concrete Foundations

The controlling requirements for foundation design are resistance to soil loads and protection from frost. Concrete walls easily support downward compressive loads, but lateral loads applied by soil pressure, and the pressures of expanding ice in the soil, can crack concrete walls. Foundation walls must be designed to resist these lateral loads.

Concrete Wall Dimensions

By code, foundation walls must always extend above the finished grade at least 6 in. However, 18 in. is recommended to prevent splashback from deteriorating wood siding. The height above grade may be lowered to 4 in. if a masonry cladding, such as brick veneer, is used.

Maximum heights of foundation walls should be based on the required wall thickness and reinforcement required, as specified below.

Concrete Wall Thickness

The design thickness of foundation walls depends on soil conditions, the amount of reinforcement in the wall, the height of the wall, and the height of unbalanced fill. *Unbalanced fill* refers to the difference in ground-level height between the inside and outside of the foundation wall.

While code will allow *plain*, or unreinforced, concrete and masonry block foundation walls (refer to **Figure R404.1.1 (1)**, p. 67 of the 2000 International Residential Code), this is not recommended. Code sets minimums for safety, not necessarily for quality. To avoid the callback nightmare of a cracked foundation, all foundations should include reinforcing steel. An exception can be made for a plain concrete or masonry foundation wall less than 5 ft. tall with less than 4 ft. of unbalanced fill. In this case, use minimum 4,000-psi concrete (see "Specifying Ready-Mix," page 30).

Figure 54. Full-Height vs. Half-Height Foundation Walls

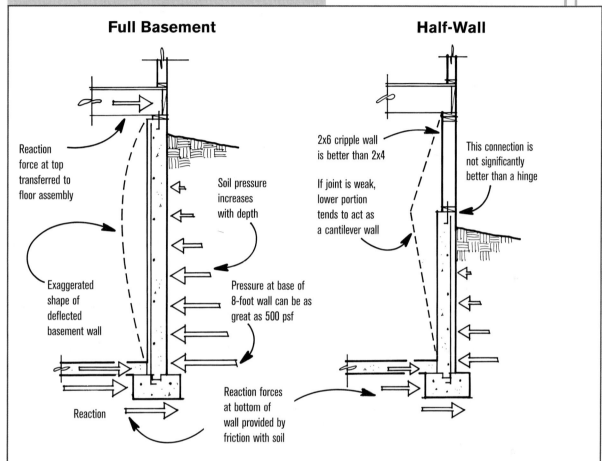

Full Basement

Reaction force at top transferred to floor assembly

Soil pressure increases with depth

Exaggerated shape of deflected basement wall

Pressure at base of 8-foot wall can be as great as 500 psf

Reaction

Reaction forces at bottom of wall provided by friction with soil

Half-Wall

2x6 cripple wall is better than 2x4

This connection is not significantly better than a hinge

If joint is weak, lower portion tends to act as a cantilever wall

A full-height foundation wall is braced at the top by floor framing and at the bottom by the concrete footing and slab, so it is likely to bow inward. Reinforcement placed towards the inside face will resist cracking caused by this bowing (left). A concrete/cripple wall combination, however, is braced only at the bottom; the connection between the concrete and the wood wall is little more than a hinge (right). To resist toppling inward, the concrete wall must be detailed like a free-standing retaining wall, with rebar placed towards the outside face.

Figure 55. Stepped Foundation Corners

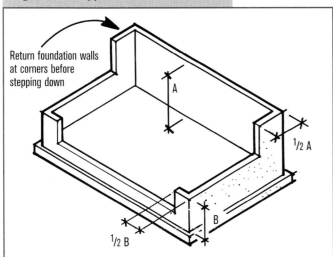

Return foundation walls at corners before stepping down

A

½ A

B

½ B

Regardless of height, every concrete wall should be braced at each corner. Maintain the higher wall height for a distance equal to half that wall height.

Typically, a foundation wall should be thicker than the wall it supports. An 8-in.-thick wall is standard for supporting wood-framed walls, but only if the unbalanced fill height is less than 6 ft., the foundation is located on a well-drained site, and the foundation is properly reinforced.

Where poor soils exist, in seismic zones, and on hillside sites, a thicker 10- or 12-in. poured concrete wall may be required. In each of these cases, an engineer's review is recommended and may be required by local code.

Reinforcing Concrete Walls

Follow general guidelines for reinforcing foundations (see "Rebar," pages 50-55).

For appropriate sizing and spacing of rebar in concrete foundations, follow the minimum code requirements shown in **Figures 47, 48,** and **49,** pages 51-54.

Rebar should always be placed near the tension side of the concrete (see "Placing Rebar in Walls," page 55). On a full-height foundation wall, which is held in place by floor framing at the top and by the footing at the bottom, the tension side is toward the inside (**Figure 46,** page 50).

Horizontal rebar is most effective along the top and bottom of the foundation elevation.

Stepped Foundation Walls

Foundation walls on sloped sites are often built as a half-wall with a wood-frame cripple wall (**Figure 54,** page 63). In a half-height foundation wall, the hinge joint between the concrete and the cripple, or pony, wall creates a structural weakness. The half-height portion of the wall must be treated as a retaining wall, and reinforced, buttressed, or otherwise supported to resist the lateral loading of unbalanced soil (see "Retaining Walls," page 81).

Stepped Foundation Corners

When any foundation wall turns a corner, maintain the height for a distance equal to half the height of the higher wall before stepping it down (**Figure 55**).

Structural Bracing for Foundation Walls

Always frame the floor deck before placing backfill. If this is not possible, install temporary bracing before placing backfill (see "Bracing Before Backfill," page 109).

Where soils impose an excessive lateral load, additional intermediate structural support for foundation walls can be provided by the cast foundation elements (**Figure 56**).

Figure 56. Cast-In Bracing for Foundation Walls

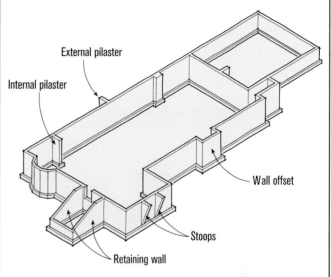

Any of the pop-outs or cast elements of a foundation wall will add lateral support, and they can be engineered to provide critical bracing of foundations in marginal soils.

Control Joints

Some surface cracking is inevitable in the face of concrete walls. Rebar and wire mesh are placed to keep cracks from widening but will not prevent them from occurring. If minor, random cracking is unacceptable, use control joints to confine cracks to intended locations.

Place control joints no more than 20 ft. apart, and within 10 ft. from corners. Locate control joints at natural points of weakness, such as door and window openings, corners, and changes in elevation or section (**Figure 57**). In a stepped foundation, control joints should also be placed along a vertical in line with the point where the foundation changes elevations.

Figure 57. Control Joints for Concrete Walls and Slabs

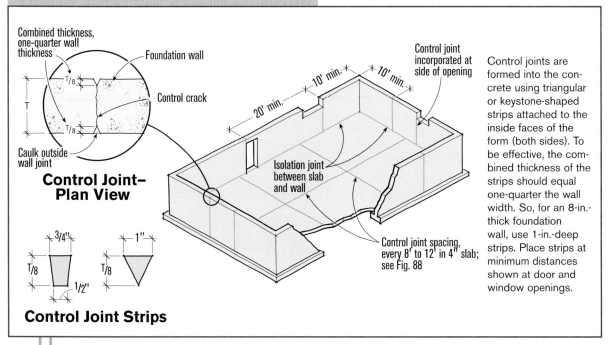

Control joints are formed into the concrete using triangular or keystone-shaped strips attached to the inside faces of the form (both sides). To be effective, the combined thickness of the strips should equal one-quarter the wall width. So, for an 8-in.-thick foundation wall, use 1-in.-deep strips. Place strips at minimum distances shown at door and window openings.

Concrete Block Foundations

Foundations built with concrete block may cost less than poured concrete, depending on local material and labor costs. Block may also be more practical than poured concrete for small jobs, crawlspace foundations, or jobs where access by concrete trucks is limited.

Block foundation performance depends on proper design and detailing. Effective perimeter drainage is a necessity to reduce lateral soil pressures, especially for full basements (see "Perimeter Foundation Drains," page 105). Block is also very porous, so waterproofing or dampproofing is usually required to control moisture intrusion (see "Waterproofing and Dampproofing," page 102).

Block Types

Most block basements are built with two-core or three-core hollow, load-bearing concrete masonry units (CMUs). Solid blocks are used to carry

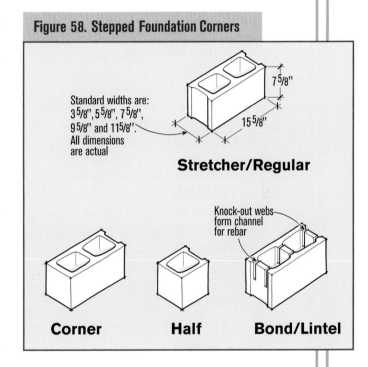

Figure 58. Stepped Foundation Corners

Standard widths are: 3 5/8", 5 5/8", 7 5/8", 9 5/8" and 11 5/8". All dimensions are actual

7 5/8"

15 5/8"

Stretcher/Regular

Knock-out webs form channel for rebar

Corner   **Half**   **Bond/Lintel**

point loads and to cap foundations. **Figure 58** shows some of the common types of block likely to be needed for building a block basement. Other specially shaped blocks are available for use in bond beams, joist and girder pockets, window and door openings, pilasters, and piers.

Setting Block in Hot Weather

Hot, dry, windy conditions speed up the setting of mortar and also cause it to dry out from evaporation. Maintaining cool and moist conditions helps reduce these problems. For improved results in hot, dry weather, take these steps:

- Adjust mortar mix. Use more cement per batch to speed strength gain so mortar will set before water evaporates out.

- Reduce mortar exposure time. Lay mortar beds no more than 4 ft. ahead, and set block within one minute.

- Keep tools and materials cool. Store block, cement, lime, and sand in the shade; if sand becomes dry, dampen it by sprinkling.

- Use cool water to mix mortar.

- Set up windscreens to deflect drying breezes.

- Cover walls with plastic as soon as possible to hold moisture in, or spray-cure walls.

Block Grades

When selecting block, choose blocks graded according to ASTM standards. Use only ASTM Grade N for foundations, not Grade S. Grade N has greater bearing strength and better resistance to frost action and moisture.

Block Types

Masonry units of ASTM Type I (moisture-controlled), rather than Type II, are recommended; Type I units are less susceptible to drying shrinkage and cracking.

Block Dimensions

Concrete block generally conforms to a modular system based on 4 in. or 8 in. Depth, height, and length of blocks are stated in full inches, but the actual dimensions are reduced by $3/8$ in. or $5/8$ in. to allow for the mortar joint. That way, walls can be designed in full lengths based on feet and inches (see "Estimating Block," page 2), and block laid with mortar joints will fall out correctly when installed.

In describing block, the wall or block width is always named first, then the course or block height, and finally the length of the block. For example, an 8x8x16-in. unit is actually $75/8$ in. thick, $7 5/8$ in. high, and $15 5/8$ in. long. Most block is available in half sizes, but odd lengths or heights may have to be cut on site.

Figure 59. Standard Mortar Mixes

Type	Cement	Lime	Sand	Compressive Strength (psi)
M	1	1/4	3	2,500
S	1	1/2	4	1,800
N	1	1	6	750
O	1	2	9	350
K	1	3	12	75

Use these ratios of ingredients for mixing different mortar types. Typically, one bag of materials (cement and lime) is equivalent to 1 cu. ft. of loose material (sand). The ratios of ingredients alter the compressive strength of the mortars, but also affect workability and bond strengths. As a rule of thumb, tensile strength is a little less than one-tenth the compressive strength.

Mortar

Mortar serves to bond the units together, accommodate minor size variations between units, and create a seal against air and moisture. Mortar may also bond with reinforcing wire placed between courses.

Grout is different from mortar. Grout is used to fill block cores for reinforcement (see "Grouting Block Foundations," page 73).

Mortar Ingredients

Mortar is made of Portland cement, hydrated lime, sand, and water. Portland cement gives mortar its compressive strength. The lime weakens the mix, but improves its workability and helps form a better seal. Sand provides strength and also reduces drying shrinkage. Water provides workability and enhances the bond to the block or brick.

Mortar Types

Mortars are graded by type, based on the proportions of the ingredients (see **Figure 59**). The five traditional mortar types are known as Type M, S, N, O, and K, in descending order of compressive strength (using every other letter from the phrase "Mason Work"). Types with higher proportions of cement and lower proportions of lime have greater compressive strengths but are less workable.

For block joints: Many skilled masons prefer Type N (a.k.a. "6-1-1") for bonding block because it has better

Figure 60. Running Bond

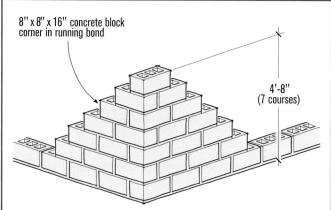

8" x 8" x 16" concrete block corner in running bond

4'-8"
(7 courses)

A running bond starts from the corner with each course offset by half a block from the one below it. By building up the corner first, a mason can establish the course heights and the plumb of the wall.

workability, allowing for a better-made joint and a better bond. The higher lime content also makes this mortar more "extensible," or flexible, in service.

For parging: Use Type M or S mortar for parging block prior to dampproofing (see "Parging Concrete Block," page 102).

Mortar Strength

Type M or Type S mortar is often specified for basement foundations because of its higher compressive strengths. However, the compressive

Setting Block in Cold Weather

Cool temperatures (below 40°F) slow the strength gain of mortar, and freezing can ruin the compressive and bond strength of mortar.

Below 40°F, take these steps:

• Heat mixing water. Maintain mortar temperature between 40°F and 120°F until placed.

• Cover work and materials. Use tarps to protect mortar, block, sand, and masonry work from wetting and freezing.

Below 32°F, add these precautions:

• Heat sand and block. Pile sand over a section of steel culvert pipe, and thaw frozen sand by directing the exhaust from a salamander heater into the pipe. Also thaw frozen block.

• Set up windbreaks or an enclosure.

• Protect work and materials. Maintain masonry and materials above 32°F with auxiliary heat or insulated blankets for 24 hours after laying block.

Below 20°F, take the following additional steps:

• Heat masonry units to 20°F or warmer.

• Provide heated enclosure for work. Keep masonry enclosure above 32°F for 24 hours after laying block.

strength of the mortar is less important than the quality of the joint and strength of the bond. (Cutting the mortar's compressive strength in half lowers the compressive strength of the total wall assembly by only about 10%.) If lateral soil loads are a concern, no mortar will provide sufficient strength. Instead, the block cores should be filled with grout and rebar (see "Reinforcing Block Foundations," page 76).

Mortar Water Content

Unlike concrete, which should be made with as little water as practical, mortar performs best when made with as much water as possible for a workable mix. Wetter mortar makes a stronger bond with the block, increasing the performance of the total wall system.

Site-Mixed Mortar

Mortar is usually mixed on site with water, Portland cement, lime, and sand. Site-mixing allows skilled masons to fine-tune the quality of the mortar, easing the labor and improving the quality of the job.

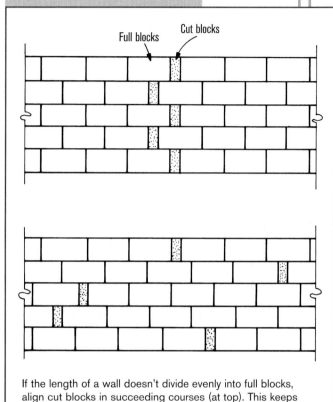

Figure 61. Cut Block Placement

Full blocks   Cut blocks

If the length of a wall doesn't divide evenly into full blocks, align cut blocks in succeeding courses (at top). This keeps the cores lined up and looks much better than random placement (at bottom).

Pre-Bagged Mortar

Pre-bagged masonry cement mixes are available, with the cement and lime pre-proportioned so that only sand and water need to be added. If unskilled help is mixing the mortar, pre-bagged cements make it easier to get a uniform mix from batch to batch.

Figure 62. Corner Layout for Block

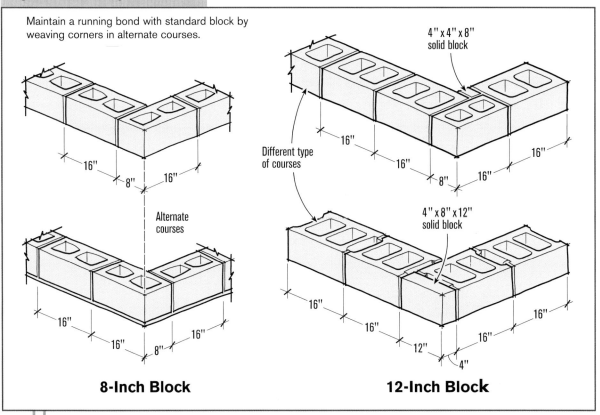

Maintain a running bond with standard block by weaving corners in alternate courses.

4" x 4" x 8" solid block

Different type of courses

Alternate courses

8-Inch Block

4" x 8" x 12" solid block

12-Inch Block

Bagged Material Weights

Bags of Portland cement, masonry cement, and lime all contain 1 cu. ft. of material per bag, although they weigh different amounts. Portland cement weighs almost 100 lbs./cu. ft.; lime weighs about 50 lbs./cu. ft.; and masonry cements— which are mixtures of Portland and lime—weigh somewhere in between, depending on the type.

Footings for Block Foundations

Footings for block walls do not differ much from cast footings for poured concrete walls (see "Footings," pages 44-49).

If block and other materials will be staged inside the building perimeter before footings are poured, take care that stored materials do not prevent you from checking cross-diagonals and measuring foundation widths.

Setting Block

As with concrete, mortar sets up best in humid climates with temperatures averaging above 40°F and below 70°F. In climate conditions above and below this, follow similar procedures described in "Hot-Weather Concrete," (page 42) and "Cold-Weather Concrete," (page 39).

Grouting Block Foundations

Grout is used to fill cores and bond beams for strength, along with appropriately sized and placed steel rebar. Grout is not the same as mortar. It is really a type of concrete, made with Portland cement, water, sand, and small crushed rock or pea gravel, but little or no lime. Grout typically reaches a compressive strength of 2,500 to 3,000 psi.

Ordering Ready-Mix Grout

Grout is best ordered from a ready-mix plant. A grout mix delivered by truck typically will be about an 8-bag concrete mix with maximum 1/2-in. gravel.

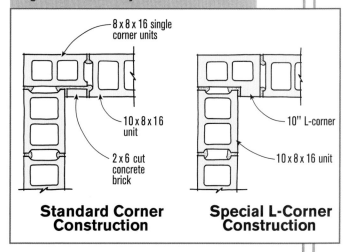

Figure 63. Corner Layout for 10-in. Block

8 x 8 x 16 single corner units

10 x 8 x 16 unit

2 x 6 cut concrete brick

10" L-corner

10 x 8 x 16 unit

Standard Corner Construction

Special L-Corner Construction

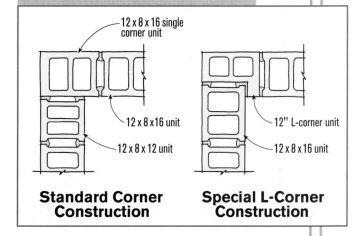

Figure 64. Corner Layout for 12-in. Block

12 x 8 x 16 single corner unit

12 x 8 x 16 unit

12 x 8 x 12 unit

12" L-corner unit

12 x 8 x 16 unit

Standard Corner Construction

Special L-Corner Construction

Site-Mixed Grout

If mixing small batches of grout on site, make sure to mix the batch for at least five minutes. Place the grout soon

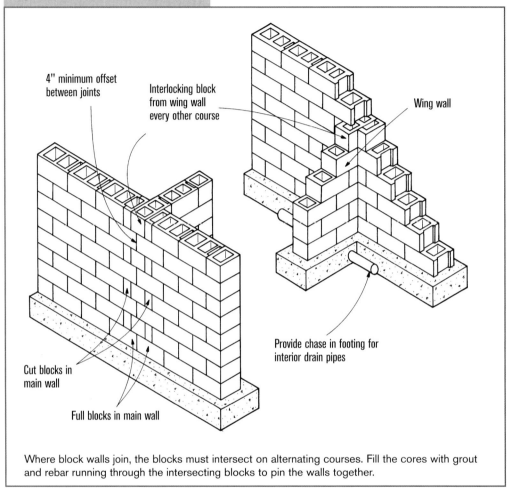

Figure 65. Intersecting Block Walls

4" minimum offset between joints

Interlocking block from wing wall every other course

Wing wall

Cut blocks in main wall

Full blocks in main wall

Provide chase in footing for interior drain pipes

Where block walls join, the blocks must intersect on alternating courses. Fill the cores with grout and rebar running through the intersecting blocks to pin the walls together.

after mixing. Discard any batch of grout that is not placed within 90 minutes.

Block Construction Details

If you have control over design decisions, lay out the distances between corners and bump-outs, as well as the dimensions of door and window openings, in increments of 8- or 16-in. to match full- and half-block lengths.

Running Bond

Concrete blocks are designed to be laid in a running bond (sometimes called half-bond) pattern in which the vertical joint of two adjoining blocks falls over the center of the block below (**Figure 60**, page 70).

Cut Block Placement

If blocks must be cut, maintain a running bond by staggering cut blocks symmetrically (**Figure 61**, page 71). Joints can be as close as 4 in. from a joint in the courses above and below and not affect the strength of the wall; but the appearance will suffer if the joints are off-center. Where portions of the wall will have cores filled with concrete, keep the half-bond dead accurate.

Building Block Corners

Corners are a key detail in a block basement, and must be built to maintain a modular layout. With 8-in. block, weaving block at corners establishes the 8-in. running bond and keeps the cores in two-core block in line (**Figure 62**, page 72). For 10- and 12-in. block, a number of techniques can be used to lay out corners (**Figures 63** and **64**, page 73); the simplest method uses special corner block.

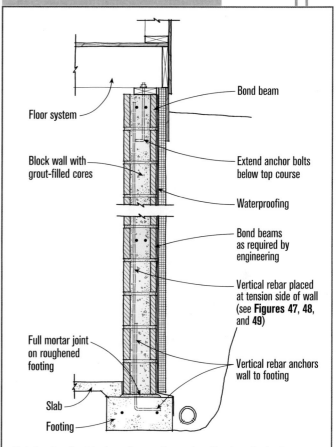

Figure 66. Reinforcing Block Walls

Bond beam · Floor system · Block wall with grout-filled cores · Extend anchor bolts below top course · Waterproofing · Bond beams as required by engineering · Vertical rebar placed at tension side of wall (see **Figures 47, 48,** and **49**) · Full mortar joint on roughened footing · Vertical rebar anchors wall to footing · Slab · Footing

Reinforcing for block walls consists primarily of vertical rebar embedded in columns of grout-filled cores to the full-height of the foundation wall. Rebar must tie to the footing, and anchor bolts must extend below the top course of block.

Concrete Block Intersections

Wall intersections add strength to help resist soil pressure. Buttresses or "wing walls" can be built to stiffen main walls even if no partition is called for (**Figure 65**).

Weave alternate courses together just as in building a corner, and grout all cores and reinforce with steel.

Figure 67. Reinforced Opening in a Block Foundation

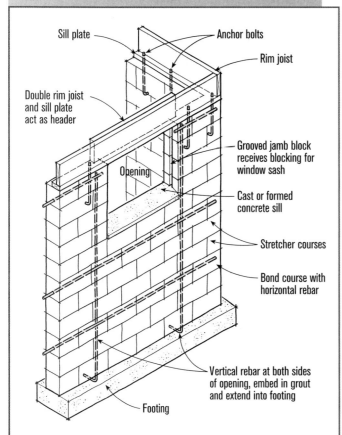

Sill plate

Anchor bolts

Rim joist

Double rim joist and sill plate act as header

Grooved jamb block receives blocking for window sash

Opening

Cast or formed concrete sill

Stretcher courses

Bond course with horizontal rebar

Vertical rebar at both sides of opening, embed in grout and extend into footing

Footing

In addition to the vertical rebar specified by code (**Figures 47, 48,** and **49**, pages 51-54), additional rebar embedded in grout should surround window openings. In an opening at the top of a foundation wall, the sill plate and floor framing act as a header and tie together the top sections of the block.

Reinforcing Block Foundations

Follow general guidelines for reinforcing foundations (see "Rebar," pages 51-55).

Rebar placed in grouted cores adds significant stiffness and strength to masonry basement walls. Place rebar towards the inside face of full-height foundation walls, and tie it securely into the footing (**Figure 66**, page 75).

For appropriate sizing and spacing of rebar in masonry foundations, follow the minimum code requirements shown in **Figures 47**, **48**, and **49** (pages 51-54).

Reinforcing Openings in Block Foundations

To prevent cracking at stress points near openings, place reinforcing steel, as shown in **Figure 67**.

Anchoring Floor Framing to Block Foundations

In most block foundations, the floor framing acts as a critical brace to stabilize the top of the block wall. First-floor decks must be securely tied to the block:

Figure 68. Tying Block to Floor Framing

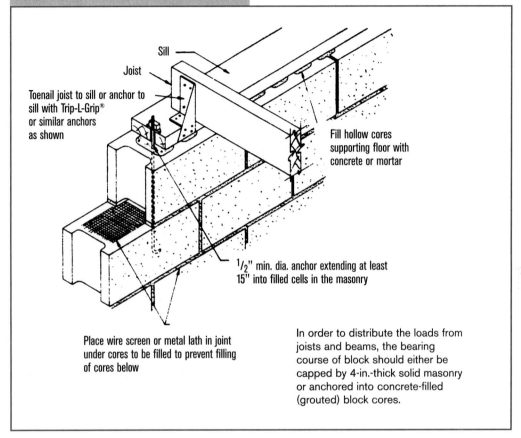

Sill

Joist

Toenail joist to sill or anchor to sill with Trip-L-Grip® or similar anchors as shown

Fill hollow cores supporting floor with concrete or mortar

$1/2$" min. dia. anchor extending at least 15" into filled cells in the masonry

Place wire screen or metal lath in joint under cores to be filled to prevent filling of cores below

In order to distribute the loads from joists and beams, the bearing course of block should either be capped by 4-in.-thick solid masonry or anchored into concrete-filled (grouted) block cores.

- Anchor bolts should be embedded at least 12 in. into grouted cores. Ideally, the core with the anchor bolt should be fully grouted down to the footing, contain vertical rebar, and be tied to the footing with a rebar dowel (**Figure 66**, page 75).

- Floor joists must be securely fastened to the sill plate with toenails or clips (**Figure 68**).

- Bracing or blocking on joists parallel to foundation wall must extend three joists back from the wall (**Figure 69**).

Bond Beams

In tall foundation walls (8 ft. or higher) a bond beam running along the top course is recommended to tie walls together, particularly in poor soil

Figure 69. Bracing Block Walls

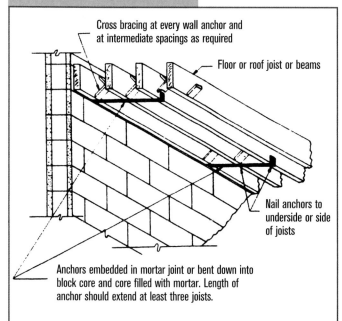

Cross bracing at every wall anchor and at intermediate spacings as required

Floor or roof joist or beams

Nail anchors to underside or side of joists

Anchors embedded in mortar joint or bent down into block core and core filled with mortar. Length of anchor should extend at least three joists.

Joists running parallel to a block wall should be braced every 8 ft. The bracing (or joist blocking) should span at least three joists.

Figure 70. Bond Beam

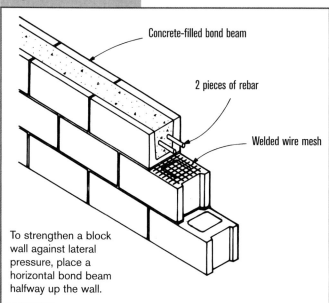

Concrete-filled bond beam

2 pieces of rebar

Welded wire mesh

To strengthen a block wall against lateral pressure, place a horizontal bond beam halfway up the wall.

conditions. On wet sites and in seismic zones, an engineer may also specify bond beams for lateral support midway in the foundation wall elevation (**Figure 70**).

To form bond beams, place rebar and pour grout in the channel made by knocking out the webs in special bond-beam block. Use two #4 bars in 8-ft. walls and two #5 bars in 10- or 12-ft. walls. Lap bars at joints, and bend bars around corners by at least 24 bar diameters.

Joint Reinforcement

Wire-mesh joint reinforcement is used to help reduce the size of cracks, but it does not add appreciable structural strength. Typically, mesh is placed in the mortar joints every second or third course (**Figure 70**).

Control Joints

Avoid using expansion and control joints in basement construction when possible because they weaken the walls in the horizontal span and increase the potential for foundation leaks.

Permanent Wood Foundations

Permanent wood foundations is the term used by the wood-treating industry, and adopted by residential building codes, for basements built with pressure-treated wood that is rated for ground contact (**Figure 71**).

Approved Pressure-Treated Wood

When buying wood for a permanent wood foundation, check the wood treater's stamp and be sure it bears the notation "C-22," which denotes a standard created by the American Wood-Preservers' Assoc. (817/326-6300, www.awpa.com) to cover foundation-grade lumber. This kind of wood typically must be special-ordered, and can be as much as twice the price of in-stock, 0.4-pcf pressure-treated lumber found in most lumberyards.

Critical Installation Details

- **Subbase:** Subbase should extend below frost line. Use gravel or crushed stone, properly compacted, under wall and slab. Subbase under perimeter walls should be at least 16 in. wide and 16 in. deep. The subbase under the slab should be at least 4 in. deep.

- **Footing plate:** Use "C-22" pressure-treated 2x8, rated for this use. All cuts in footing plates or any other lumber must be field-treated with preservative.

- **Bottom plate:** Use "C-22" pressure-treated 2x6.

- **Wall framing:** Use "C-22" pressure-treated 2x6 studs, framed 16 in. o.c. or 12 in. o.c., depending on load.

- **Sheathing:** Use pressure-treated plywood.

- **Insulation:** Use fiberglass batts, leaving a 2-in. gap between insulation and exterior wall, and install a vapor barrier on the warm side.

Figure 71. Permanent Wood Foundation

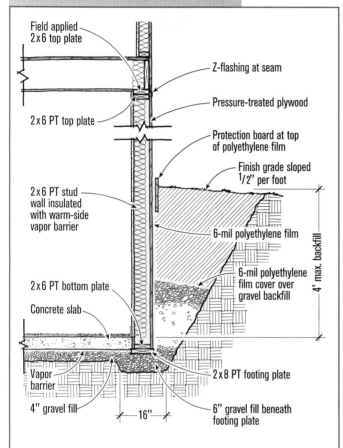

Field applied
2x6 top plate

Z-flashing at seam

Pressure-treated plywood

2x6 PT top plate

Protection board at top
of polyethylene film

Finish grade sloped
1/2" per foot

2x6 PT stud
wall insulated
with warm-side
vapor barrier

6-mil polyethylene film

6-mil polyethylene
film cover over
gravel backfill

2x6 PT bottom plate

4' max. backfill

Concrete slab

Vapor
barrier

2x8 PT footing plate

4" gravel fill

16"

6" gravel fill beneath
footing plate

Where soil conditions permit, a permanent wood foundation may be an inexpensive foundation alternative. Frame the foundation only with "C-22" pressure-treated wood approved for ground contact.

- **Waterproofing:** Use a 6-mil polyethylene film on sheathing exterior, terminated at grade. Protect termination with treated plywood or 1-in. treated lumber. Place poly over sheathing and perimeter-drainage gravel before placing soil backfill.

- **Floor slab:** Pour 4-in. concrete, placed before backfilling.

- **First floor deck:** Build in accordance with code, framed before backfilling. (Note: Backfilling before floor deck and slab are in place is likely to cause damage or collapse.)

- **Backfill:** Use only gravel at perimeter (approximately 16 in. deep above footing plate and brought up to within 12 in. of the finish grade); remaining backfill may be native soil. Total depth of backfill must not exceed 4 ft.

Retaining Walls

Retaining walls hold back the pressure of earth embankments. Unlike basement walls, they are not braced at the top by a floor system, and must be designed so they will not topple or fail in bending at the bottom.

Figure 72. Forces in a Retaining Wall

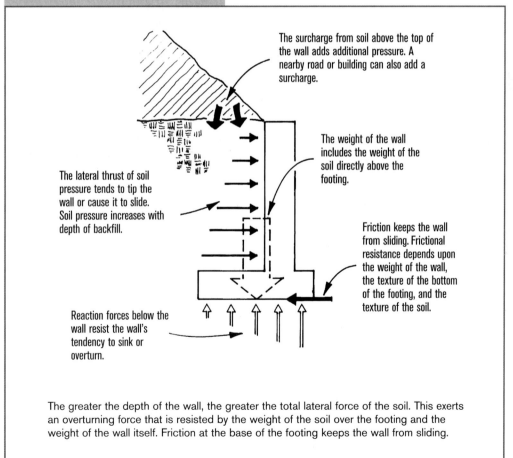

The surcharge from soil above the top of the wall adds additional pressure. A nearby road or building can also add a surcharge.

The weight of the wall includes the weight of the soil directly above the footing.

The lateral thrust of soil pressure tends to tip the wall or cause it to slide. Soil pressure increases with depth of backfill.

Friction keeps the wall from sliding. Frictional resistance depends upon the weight of the wall, the texture of the bottom of the footing, and the texture of the soil.

Reaction forces below the wall resist the wall's tendency to sink or overturn.

The greater the depth of the wall, the greater the total lateral force of the soil. This exerts an overturning force that is resisted by the weight of the soil over the footing and the weight of the wall itself. Friction at the base of the footing keeps the wall from sliding.

Engineering

Doubling the soil height quadruples the pressure, so any retaining wall higher than 4 ft. should be designed by an engineer. If vehicle loads or other heavy loads will be placed above a wall, it should also be engineered.

Railings

Some codes require safety railings on any retaining wall higher than 30 in., whether there is a walkway or not. Typically, railings must be 42 in. high.

Forces in a Retaining Wall

Soil pressure on a retaining wall increases with increasing depth (**Figure 72**, page 81). Walls can fail in bending, by sliding, or by toppling. When engineering a wall, all three failure modes must be analyzed.

Drainage for Retaining Walls

Soil pressures on a retaining wall increase drastically when the soil is saturated (see "Soils," page 3). At the same time, the chance of soils sliding or overturning increases when soil is wet. Backfilling with poorly draining material, or failing to provide positive

Figure 73. Rebar in Concrete Retaining Walls

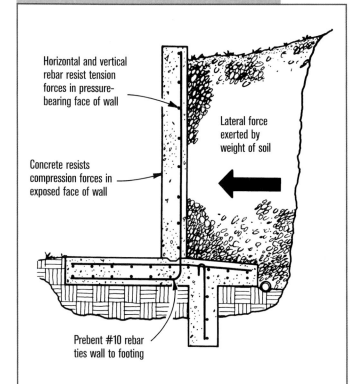

Horizontal and vertical rebar resist tension forces in pressure-bearing face of wall

Lateral force exerted by weight of soil

Concrete resists compression forces in exposed face of wall

Prebent #10 rebar ties wall to footing

The compressive strength of concrete and the tensile strength of steel work together to resist lateral pressures placed on a retaining wall.

Figure 74. Masonry Retaining Walls

Poured Concrete

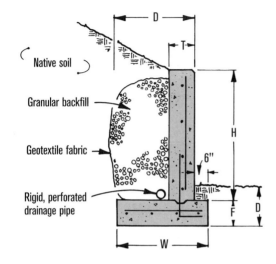

Concrete Block

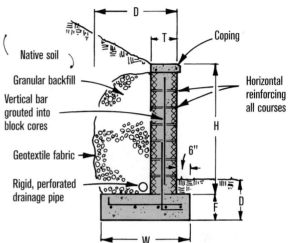

Mortared or Dry-Laid Stone

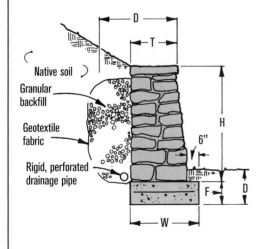

Recommended Dimensions for Low Masonry Retaining Walls*

H	W	Steel Rebar	Bar Spacing	F	T	D
2'	20"	#3 ($3/8$")	2'-0" o.c.	9"	8"	Local frost depth or 12" to 18"
3'	25"	#4 ($1/2$")	2'-0" o.c.	10"	8"	
4'	32"	#5 ($5/8$")	2'-0" o.c.	11"	10"	
5'	42"	#5 ($5/8$")	1'-6" o.c.	12"	12"	

* Suggested details for walls no higher than 5 ft. where dense, coarse-grain soil exists below footings. Not for loose or soft sand, peat, or clay.

Figure 75. Timber Retaining Walls

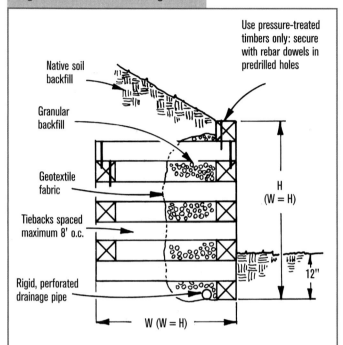

Use pressure-treated timbers only: secure with rebar dowels in predrilled holes

Native soil backfill

Granular backfill

Geotextile fabric

Tiebacks spaced maximum 8' o.c.

Rigid, perforated drainage pipe

H (W = H)

12"

W (W = H)

Recommended Dimensions for Low Timber Crib Walls*

Timber Size	Dowel Size	Spacing of Tiebacks
6x6	1/2" (#4 bar)**	6'-0" (max.)
8x8	3/4" (#6 bar)**	8'-0" (max.)

* Details apply to walls no higher than 5 ft.

** In acidic soils, increase by 1/4 in. or use hot-dipped galvanized.

drainage, greatly increases the odds of wall failure. Always backfill retaining walls with free-draining granular material (sand or gravel), and provide drains that allow water to escape from behind walls (see "Drainage," page 105).

Reinforcing Retaining Walls

Follow general guidelines for reinforcing foundations (see "Rebar," page 50).

In a retaining wall, which is not braced at the top like a foundation wall, steel goes on the side of the wall close to the soil load, where tensile stresses occur (**Figure 73**, page 82).

Poured Concrete and Masonry Retaining Walls

For concrete and masonry retaining walls less than 5-ft.-tall, follow guidelines for steel placement and dimensions as shown in **Figure 74**, page 83. Taller walls should be designed by a qualified engineer.

Timber Retaining Walls

Crib walls built out of landscaping ties function like a gravity wall. The mass of earth in the crib structure holds back the pressure of the soil behind it. Wood must be treated against rot. Timbers can be joined with 10- or 11-in.-long, hot-dipped, galvanized spikes or with rebar dowels in pre-drilled holes.

Crib walls can be as high as 30 ft., but a qualified engineer should design walls higher than 5 ft. For walls 5 ft. or shorter, follow the guidelines shown in **Figure 75**.

Tiebacks for Low Walls

For very low timber retaining walls in granular soil, you may be able to use tiebacks instead of an actual crib design (see **Figure 76**). Tiebacks spaced 16 ft. o.c., staggered on alternate courses, are typical. (For greater holding power, space tiebacks closer.) Tiebacks should extend into soil a distance equal to the wall height.

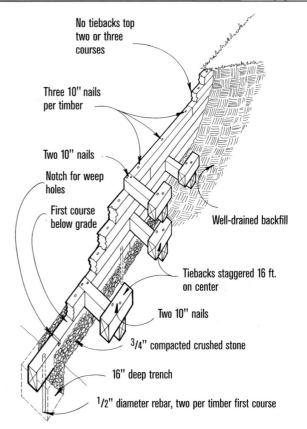

Figure 76. Tiebacks for Low Retaining Walls

No tiebacks top two or three courses

Three 10" nails per timber

Two 10" nails

Notch for weep holes

First course below grade

Well-drained backfill

Tiebacks staggered 16 ft. on center

Two 10" nails

3/4" compacted crushed stone

16" deep trench

1/2" diameter rebar, two per timber first course

T-shaped timber tiebacks every 16 ft. on each course help to stabilize very low timber walls. In heavy soils, backfill with sand or crushed stone. With new, surfaced timbers that fit snugly together, weep holes or perforated drain pipe is needed to relieve hydrostatic pressure.

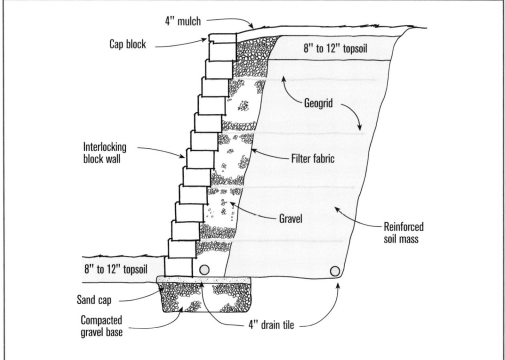

Figure 77. Interlocking Block Retaining Walls

4" mulch

Cap block

8" to 12" topsoil

Geogrid

Interlocking block wall

Filter fabric

Gravel

Reinforced soil mass

8" to 12" topsoil

Sand cap

Compacted gravel base

4" drain tile

In an interlocking block wall, geogrid is typically placed on soil layers at 1- to 2-ft. intervals, and the soil is compacted in lifts. Block without geogrid may be sufficient for walls up to 4 ft. in height; with geogrid, walls can be as high as 16 ft. or more.

Interlocking Block Retaining Walls

Geogrid is a plastic grid material used to reinforce soil banks. In combination with interlocking block systems, it can be used to create a block-faced earth retaining wall that functions similarly to a concrete gravity retaining wall (**Figure** 77).

Engineered Tall Walls

A qualified engineer should design block walls higher than 5 ft. Usually, the vertical spacing of the geogrid is about twice the depth of the masonry units, and the geogrid extends into the soil horizontally a distance equal to 60% to 80% the total wall height, depending on the surcharge above the wall.

Slabs

Site Layout for Slab Foundations

When framing a floor system, there is a little latitude in both the timing and installation of the utilities. But when building on a slab, the utilities must be defined precisely before any concrete is poured.

Plumbers First

When starting layout, make sure the plumber is the first trade on site. Let other subs work around him — it's a lot easier for an electrician to work around obstructions than it is for the plumber.

Before excavation begins, work through the plumbing plans to define

---

Slab Layout Checklist

Keep careful track of these critical layout details for structural slabs:

- **Benchmark:** A slab excavation should be as level as possible. Set an elevation benchmark prior to excavation. Place the benchmark somewhere convenient and make sure everybody on the site knows where it is (**Figure 79**, page 89).

- **Concrete formwork:** Form monolithic slabs as shown in **Figure 78**, page 88. Double-check forms, verifying that they are located properly, both in relation to the corner points the surveyor set prior to excavation and in relation to the elevation benchmark.

- **Reference lines:** Mark on the edge of forms one reference point from which each sub-trade can take dimensions and work. A string line across the forms is ideal. Locate this reference line at some feature of the building that cannot change, such as the longest bearing wall. Make sure that all trades clearly understand how this line corresponds to their work.

- **Edge of slab/wall:** Take time to understand the relationship between the edge of the form and the edge of the wall. Explain it to the plumber and other subs (**Figure 80**, page 90).

- **Penetrations:** Double-check all penetrations before the slab is poured. These include toilet flanges, drain boxes, turn-ups for water, electric, gas, phone, and floor drains.

Figure 78. Forming a Structural Slab

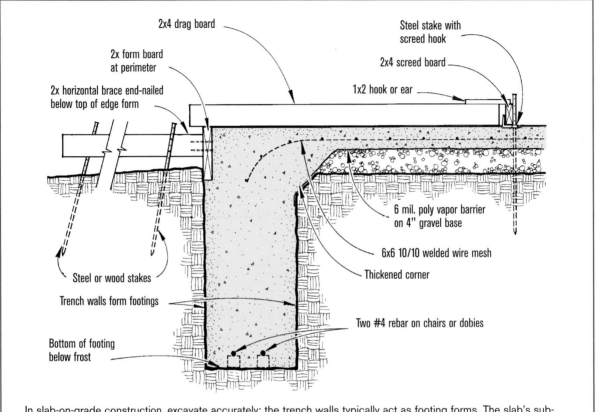

2x4 drag board

Steel stake with
screed hook

2x form board
at perimeter

2x4 screed board

2x horizontal brace end-nailed
below top of edge form

1x2 hook or ear

Steel or wood stakes

Trench walls form footings

Bottom of footing
below frost

6 mil. poly vapor barrier
on 4" gravel base

6x6 10/10 welded wire mesh

Thickened corner

Two #4 rebar on chairs or dobies

In slab-on-grade construction, excavate accurately; the trench walls typically act as footing forms. The slab's sub-base should be a minimum 4-in. compacted gravel base.

all drain/waste and supply lines and vent stack locations, and review plans for all utilities running below the slab, such as electric, gas, and phone lines.

Subslab Utilities

After the service lines have been installed, all plastic or copper lines should be properly bedded (clean fill, no rocks) and tested for leaks prior to backfilling. All copper should be checked for dents or abrasions and wrapped in split-foam insulation, or something similar, to protect it.

Install caution tape: Make sure every trade buries color-coded caution tape 12 in. below grade and in line with their work (**Figure 81**, page 91).

Figure 79. Structural Slab Layout and Formwork

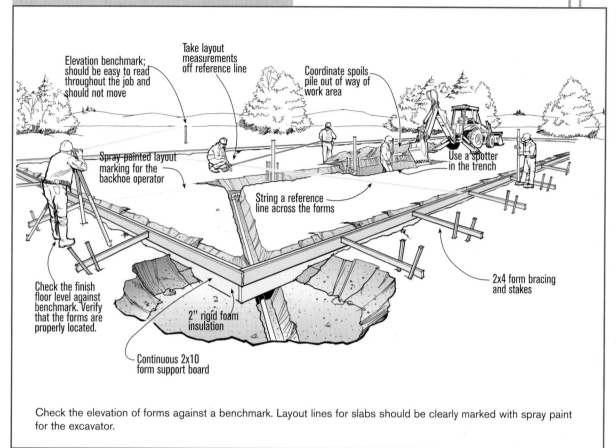

Elevation benchmark; should be easy to read throughout the job and should not move

Take layout measurements off reference line

Coordinate spoils pile out of way of work area

Spray-painted layout marking for the backhoe operator

String a reference line across the forms

Use a spotter in the trench

Check the finish floor level against benchmark. Verify that the forms are properly located.

2x4 form bracing and stakes

2" rigid foam insulation

Continuous 2x10 form support board

Check the elevation of forms against a benchmark. Layout lines for slabs should be clearly marked with spray paint for the excavator.

These plastic caution tapes are color coded: red for electric, blue for water, green for sewer, yellow for gas, and orange for phone.

Mark location of new work: Use spray paint to color-code the location of new work after backfilling trenches. It's easy to forget where lines run a few days after a trench has been backfilled.

Don't leave anything to memory: Before the concrete trucks show up, make notes either on the drawings or in a site log.

Subgrade and Subbase

Subgrade material should consist of well-drained native soil. If soils are

Figure 80. Slab/Wall Relationship

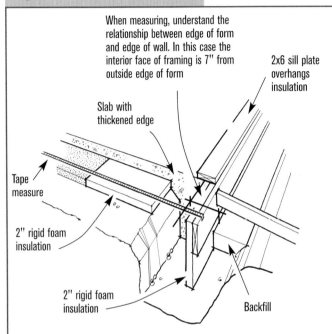

When measuring, understand the relationship between edge of form and edge of wall. In this case the interior face of framing is 7" from outside edge of form

2x6 sill plate overhangs insulation

Slab with thickened edge

Tape measure

2" rigid foam insulation

2" rigid foam insulation

Backfill

When measuring formwork, the layout crew must understand the relationship between the edge of the form and the edge of the wall. In this case, the interior face of framing is 7 in. from the outside edge of the form.

and decomposed organic material will leave voids (see "Soils," pages 3-11).

Base Compaction

Residential slabs, even with steel reinforcement, cannot span over voids or soft spots (the amount of steel used is not enough for structural reinforcement unless designed for that purpose by an engineer). Compact subgrade and subbase after utility trenching to prevent settlement, and under footings to provide even bearing strength.

Compaction is usually expressed as a percentage at optimal moisture content — usually 95% or greater (see "Compacting Soil," page 10). Run a plate tamper or jumping jack until there is very little impression left with each successive pass.

All fill material should be reasonably free of moisture, but if it's too dry, you can pound on it all day and it won't compact much. In this case, spray it sparingly with water.

Level Base

The subbase must be graded to the same level across the full width of the slab. Level the subbase to within 1/2 in.

not suitable, excavate and replace with a deep subbase layer of compacted gravel.

Granular fill, such as gravel or a mixture of sand and gravel, works best as a subbase under a slab because it compacts well (**Figure 78**, page 88). The fill should be completely thawed and free of organic material — melted ice (less than 12.4% of a 4-in. slab). Where subgrade elevation is inconsistent, the slab will vary in thickness. This variation will cause it to cure unevenly, which will stress the concrete, increasing the likelihood of cracking.

Subslab Vapor Barriers

Install a subslab vapor barrier on interior slabs to keep moisture and soil gases from entering the home. Use a minimum 4-mil to 6-mil poly. For best results, use a cross-woven poly. Lap seams by at least 6 in.

Capillary Break

An optional 3- to 4-in. layer of sand or gravel over the poly, directly under the slab, helps reduce concrete curling and cracking by allowing water to escape from the slab at the bottom as well as the top (**Figure 82**). Damp sand is typical, but gravel or a sand-gravel mix can also be used.

Concrete for Structural Slabs

Depending on the slab's purpose, use a 3,000-psi to 4,000-psi mix (**Figure 83**, page 92) at a 4-in. slump (for

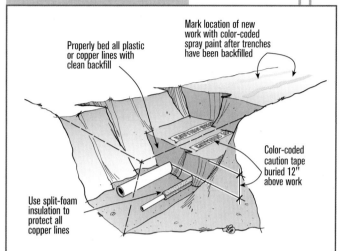

Figure 81. Utility Trench Infill

Properly bed all plastic or copper lines with clean backfill

Mark location of new work with color-coded spray paint after trenches have been backfilled

Color-coded caution tape buried 12" above work

Use split-foam insulation to protect all copper lines

Water supply lines must be below the frostline outside the foundation perimeter, and should be protected with split foam insulation throughout. Clearly mark all utility lines with caution tape 12 in. below grade, and transfer these markings to the surface with spray paint using color-coded caution tape: Red = Electric; Blue = Water; Green = Sewer; Yellow = Gas; Orange = Phone.

increased workability, consider a water-reducing admixture). For a harder surface, use a 6-bag mix. For more information on concrete mixes, see "Concrete," pages 30-43).

Use air-entrained concrete for slabs exposed to freezing.

Figure 82. Capillary Break Beneath Slabs

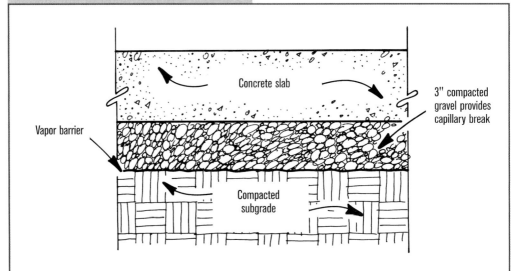

To prevent a slab from curling, use a 3-in.-thick layer of sand or gravel over the poly vapor barrier. Compact the sand before pouring the slab. While sand is more commonly used, gravel works better than sand because it is less likely to mix with the concrete or to create thin spots in the slab.

Figure 83. Concrete for Slabs

Floor Class	Application	Minimum Thickness	28-day Strength	Slump
1	Residential or tile covered	4"	3,000 psi	4"
2	Offices, churches, hospitals, schools, ornamental residential	4"	3,500 psi	4"
3	Drives, sidewalks for residences, garage floors	4"	3,500 psi	4"
4	Business or commercial walks	5"	3,500 psi	4"
5	Light industrial and commercial	5"	4,000 psi	3"

Structural Reinforcement for Slabs

Increase the thickness of a slab to 8 in. under bearing walls and structural columns (**Figure 84**).

In thickened bearing pads and exterior wall footings, lay two #4 rebars (see "Rebar," page 50).

Under a fireplace, thicken the slab to 12 in. and use #5 reinforcing bars, placed 12 in. o.c. each way to form a gridwork.

Steel Reinforcement for Slabs

To limit cracking, residential slabs require steel reinforcement — either rebar or welded wire. This steel does not increase the load-carrying strength unless purposely engineered to do so.

Rebar

In the field of a slab, use #3 or #4 rebar at 16 in. o.c. Place rebar in the center of the slab section. Use dobies or wire chairs to hold the steel off the ground. Do not use brick to support rebar, because it will pull moisture out of the surrounding concrete too quickly, creating a stress point.

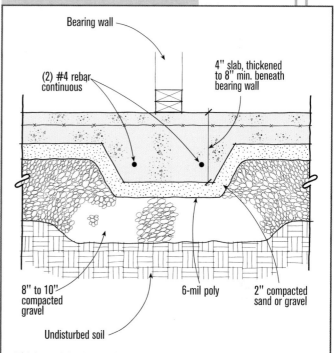

Figure 84. Slab Bearing Support

Bearing wall

(2) #4 rebar continuous

4" slab, thickened to 8" min. beneath bearing wall

8" to 10" compacted gravel

6-mil poly

2" compacted sand or gravel

Undisturbed soil

Thicken slabs beneath interior bearing walls and columns to a minimum of 8 in., using two #4 rebar about 2 in. from the bottom surface. The bearing width of all footings varies according to soil strengths and loading conditions, as shown in **Figure 40**, page 46.

Pipe or conduit laid directly on the ground will dramatically weaken the slab by effectively creating a score line on the bottom (tension) surface.

Welded-Wire Mesh

To effectively limit cracks, 6x6 wire mesh in slabs should be placed in the upper part of the slab, where cracks are

Figure 85. Crack Control Joints

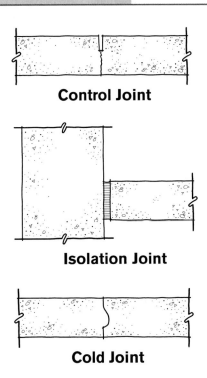

Control Joint

Isolation Joint

Cold Joint

Control joints **(center)** extend only partially into the slab surface and determine where cracks will form. Isolation, or expansion, joints **(top)** extend all the way through the slab and allow sections to slide back and forth without cracking. Cold joints **(bottom)** are necessary when a pour must be interrupted, and should coincide with control joints.

at joints. Instead, stop the mesh several inches back from the joint location.

If control joints are spaced close together, and a low-slump mix is used, wire mesh is probably not necessary.

Control Joints for Slabs

Three kinds of joints are used in concrete slabs (**Figure 85**):

- **Control joints** confine cracks to intended locations
- **Isolation joints** allow structural and non-structural elements to move separately
- **Cold, or construction, joints** define where a concrete pour has been interrupted

Cutting Control Joints

Control joints can be tooled in the slab surface with a grooving trowel or cut with an abrasive or diamond circular-saw blade at recommended spacing and depths (**Figure 86**). Make tooled joints during finishing, as soon as bleed water has evaporated. Cut sawn joints as soon as possible after finishing the slab. Random cracks may appear as rapidly as within six hours in hot weather.

noticeable, but no closer than 2 in. to the top surface. Use dobies or wire chairs to hold the steel off the ground.

At slab edges, curve the mesh down into the perimeter footings (**Figure 78**, page 88). Do not lap wire sections

Isolation Joints

Provide isolation, or expansion, joints at garage and basement slab edges (**Figure 87**) and at column footings (**Figure 88**). This prevents movement of one element from damaging the other. Expansion joints can be made of asphalt-impregnated fiberboard or a plastic strip that can be zipped off after concrete is placed.

For a finished appearance in slabs, score fiberboard expansion material prior to placing, so it can be snapped out and the joint sealed with caulk (**Figure 89**). This same detail should be employed with exterior driveway expansion joints; in this case, the caulk provides an important protection from potential freeze-thaw damage (see "Concrete Driveways," page 28).

Basement slabs must also be isolated from the footing, either with sand (**Figure 94**, page 102) or with 15# felt (**Figure 87**).

Figure 86. Control Joints for Slabs

Slab Thickness (in.)	Joint Spacing (ft.)	Joint Depth (in.)
4	8 to 12	$3/4$ to 1
5	10 to 15	1 to $1^1/4$
6	12 to 18	$1^1/4$ to $1^1/2$
7	14 to 21	$1^3/8$ to $1^3/4$
8	16 to 24	$1^5/8$ to 2
9	18 to 27	$1^3/4$ to $2^1/4$

Figure 87. Isolating Basement Slabs

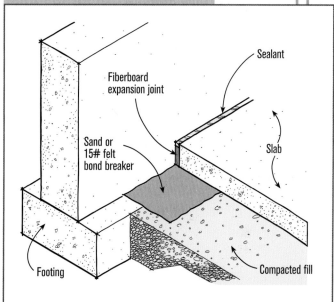

An expansion joint should be installed at the edges of a basement slab, and a bond breaker should be installed between the footing and the slab to help prevent cracking as the slab moves.

Figure 88. Isolating Column Footings

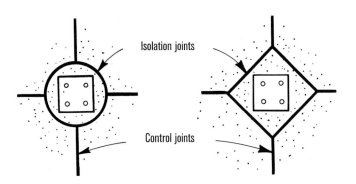

Isolation joints

Control joints

Structural columns must be isolated from the slab using block-outs that extend through the slab thickness (**Figure 85**, page 94). When forming square block-outs, align the points of the square to meet control joints.

Figure 89. Finished Expansion Joint

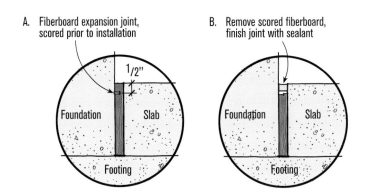

A. Fiberboard expansion joint, scored prior to installation

B. Remove scored fiberboard, finish joint with sealant

1/2"

Foundation   Slab

Footing

Foundation   Slab

Footing

For a finished appearance at the slab edge, score the fiberboard on a table saw so the top $1/2$ in. can be easily snapped off after the pour. Then finish the joint with sealant.

Pier Foundations

Pier-and-grade-beam foundations can be as simple as a sonotube foundation for a porch or small addition, or as complex as an engineered foundation for expansive soils.

Simple Pier Foundations

Simple pier-and-grade-beam foundations can support decks, porches, pole barns, and small home additions, providing good insulation and ventilation (**Figure 90**).

Sizing Piers

For sizing pier diameters for small foundations, the rule of thumb is "1 inch per foot of span." Thus, a deck that spans 8 ft. will stand comfortably on 8-in.-diameter piers, while a deck that spans 10 ft. requires 10-in.-diameter piers. For spans longer than 12 ft., add a second row of piers and a second girder at the center of the joist span.

For calculating concrete amounts, see "Estimating Concrete for Piers," page 2.

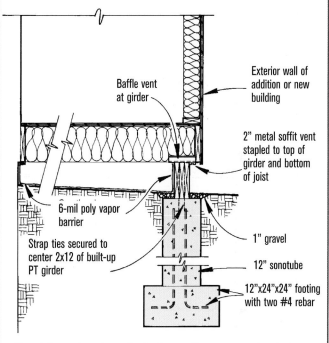

Figure 90. Simple Pier Foundations

Baffle vent at girder

Exterior wall of addition or new building

2" metal soffit vent stapled to top of girder and bottom of joist

6-mil poly vapor barrier

Strap ties secured to center 2x12 of built-up PT girder

1" gravel

12" sonotube

12"x24"x24" footing with two #4 rebar

Sonotubes, placed on pier footings with a pressure-treated grade beam, can be installed easily without disturbing existing utility lines.

Pier Footings

Footings for shallow piers (less than 6 ft. deep) will help prevent the pier from settling. The pier footing should be as thick as the pier's diameter, with sides that measure twice that much. So

Figure 91. Engineered Pier Foundation

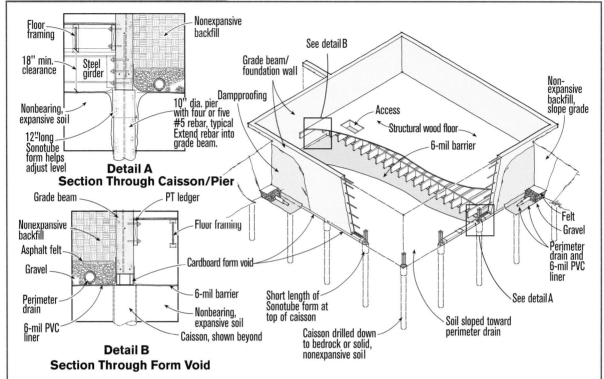

Detail A
Section Through Caisson/Pier

Detail B
Section Through Form Void

Unlike a continuous poured foundation, the heavily reinforced walls (the grade-beams) of this engineered pier foundation are isolated from the underlying soil, except where they bear on caissons that extend far below expansive soils to bedrock or more stable soils. Cardboard form voids **(Detail B)** provide temporary support when pouring the walls, but give way without stressing the foundation when expansive soils swell.

an 8-in. pier, for example, should rest on a footing that's 8 in. thick and 16 in. square, while a 12-in. pier should rest on a footing that's 12 in. thick and 24 in. square.

Simple Pier Foundation Details

• Use strap ties to anchor piers to a triple pressure-treated 2-by girder. The ties wrap around the center stick in the built-up girder and lap over the top. (The girder looks better if the ties aren't exposed on its face.)

• Install a poly vapor barrier over the ground beneath the joists, and run it up and staple it to the inside of the girder. This helps prevent water vapor from building up in the shallow space beneath the joists.

- Additional moisture control can be added by cantilevering joists 2 in. beyond the rim of the girder and installing a 2-in.-wide standard metal soffit vent on the underside of the overhanging joists.

- Finished grade should slope well away from a pier foundation — about a slope of 4 in. in 10 ft.

Engineered Pier Foundations

Pier-and-grade-beam foundations work where slopes are too steep for conventional stepped footings, where soils are weak, or where expansive soils would move conventional footings (**Figure 91**). Piers can penetrate deep through unstable soils and reach stronger soil or rock, where a combination of end bearing and soil friction against the sides of the pier supports the weight of the house. Grade beams transfer house loads onto the piers.

Engineering

A soils engineer and a structural engineer are generally necessary to design

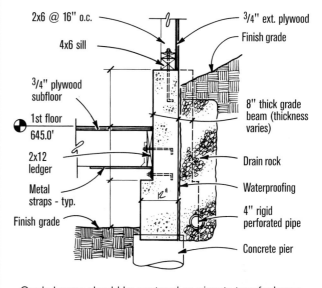

Figure 92. Grade-Beam Section

2x6 @ 16" o.c.
4x6 sill
3/4" plywood subfloor
1st floor 645.0'
2x12 ledger
Metal straps - typ.
Finish grade
3/4" ext. plywood
Finish grade
8" thick grade beam (thickness varies)
Drain rock
Waterproofing
4" rigid perforated pipe
Concrete pier
12"

Grade-beams should be centered on piers to transfer house loads directly to the piers. Provide well-draining backfill and perimeter drains to relieve soil pressure on the beam between piers.

this type of foundation and to supervise or inspect construction.

Pier Dimensions

Depth and diameter of piers are calculated based on soil characteristics and building loads. Piers may be anywhere from 5- to 20- ft. deep or deeper, depending on site conditions. Pier diameters are typically 10- to 12- in. Piers are generally spaced from 5- to

Figure 93. Pier-to-Grade-Beam

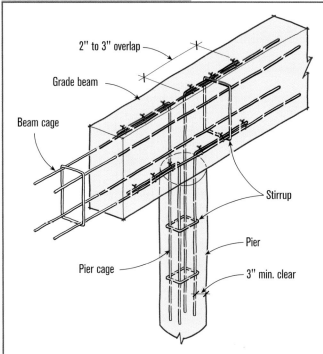

2" to 3" overlap

Grade beam

Beam cage

Stirrup

Pier

Pier cage

3" min. clear

Bend rebar to overlap rebar cages in the piers and the grade beam. Each overlap should be at least 24 bar diameters at splices and spliced tightly with wire.

(**Figure 91**, page 98), depending on loads and spans. A grade-beam may slope to conform to site contours, in which case a pony wall is typically framed over the beam (see **Figure 54**, page 63).

Reinforcement

Reinforcing steel must also be sized and installed in accordance with engineering calculations. Large (12-in.-diameter) piers should have at least four pieces of vertical rebar, creating rebar cages that tie into horizontal rebar in the beams (**Figure 93**).

Void Forms

If soils are expansive, space must be created under the beams to allow soil to expand without stressing the structure. This is accomplished with cardboard boxes placed at the bottom of the form (**Figure 91**, page 98). In less extreme cases, expanded foam (not extruded) can be used to form beams; the spaces in the foam will give a little to absorb slight expansions.

12-ft. apart. Of course, in seismic zones, on steep sites, and in areas with extreme soil conditions, these dimensions can be much greater.

Grade-Beam Dimensions

Beams are generally a minimum of 6 in. wide and 12 in. deep (**Figure 92**, page 99), but can be much larger

Anchor Bolts

Anchor bolts should be cast into the beams. In places where cripple walls are needed above grade-beams to create a level elevation for floor framing, the spacing between anchor bolts may need to be closer than usual (consult the engineer on this detail). In addition, horizontal anchor bolts may be required to secure the rim joist of floor framing **(Figure 92)**.

Backfill

Grade-beams should be backfilled with a well-compacted granular fill, and perimeter drainage should be installed that drains to daylight (see "Drainage," page 105).

Pier Foundation Details

- **Pier tops must be clean when beams are cast**. Dirt or debris between the pier and the beam can weaken the joint.

- **Soil variations can affect the bearing strength of individual piers**. If soil color or consistency changes during drilling, alert the engineer: Pier depth may have to be increased if weaker soils are encountered. Piers that are too shallow are a common source of failure.

- **Locate beams accurately on centers of piers**. Off-center beams can crack piers.

- **Maintain coverage of rebar within piers and beams**. Rebar in piers must be protected by at least 3 in. of concrete coverage. Use dobies or wire spacers to maintain distance between piers and sides of hole (engineer should check this detail). Coverage in beams must be as specified in engineer's drawings (minimum 2 in.).

Waterproofing and Dampproofing

Waterproofing refers to a continuous membrane covering that will resist water under hydrostatic pressure (i.e., standing water). *Dampproofing* is a water-resistant coating designed to shed water and resist soil moisture. Dampproofing is not effective against water under pressure.

Dampproofing

A simple dampproof coating is sufficient where positive drainage is reliable, the seasonal water table never rises above the footing, or the basement is not living space.

Dampproofing Concrete Block Basements

Spray-applied waterproofing and some waterproofing membranes can be applied directly to concrete block. However, dampproofing should be applied over parging.

Parging Concrete Block

Before parging walls, brush off any dirt and dampen wall with a water spray (do not soak).

To parge walls, trowel on two coats of Type M or S mortar. Each coat should be at least $1/4$ in. thick, for a total

Figure 94. Parging for Concrete Block Foundation

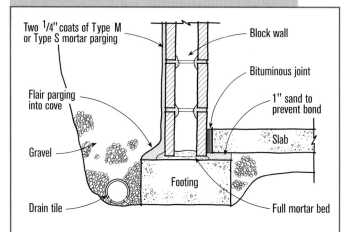

Two $1/4$" coats of Type M or Type S mortar parging

Block wall

Bituminous joint

Flair parging into cove

1" sand to prevent bond

Gravel

Slab

Footing

Drain tile

Full mortar bed

Parging should be applied to block foundations before applying a dampproof coating. At the bottom of the wall, flare the parging into a cove to shed water from the footing/wall joint.

minimum thickness of $1/2$ in. Roughen the first coat with a brush when the wall is partially dry to ensure good bonding.

Allow the first coat to harden for 24 hours before applying the second coat. Cure the topcoat for 48 hours before applying dampproofing.

Form the parging into a cove where the wall meets the footing to direct water away from the joint (**Figure 94**).

Waterproofing

Apply waterproofing products in the following situations: When soils are slow draining; basement walls are below the water table; drainage is unreliable; or the basement encloses habitable space (**Figure 95**).

Drainage Panels

Some waterproofing systems employ a dimpled or expanded-fiber geomat fastened against the foundation, either with or without an additional coating material applied to the foundation wall. These drainage panels provide an immediate break in hydrostatic pressure, carrying water from the backfill into the perimeter drains.

Figure 95. Types of Waterproofing

Type	Suppliers and Brands	Pros	Cons	Comments
Liquid Membranes	Tremco Barrier Solutions' Tuff-N-Dri (spray-applied polymer-modified asphalt); Tremco's Tremproof 60 and Pecora's Duramem 500 (polyurethane liquid membranes for trowel, roller, or spray application)	Quick application	Possible inconsistency in coverage, 60-mil min. required	Follow manufacturer's recommended procedures carefully for voids and joints. Cement cove or fillet may be needed at footing-wall corner. Monitor coverage.
Sheet Membranes	W.R. Grace's Bituthene, Pecora's Duramem 700-SM, and W.R. Meadows' Sealtight and Mel-Rol	Consistent thickness, easy patching of holes, "fish-mouths," puckers, and wrinkles	High cost, tricky to use (sticks to everything)	Many details to learn – e.g., surface preparation, priming, patching, joint treatment, terminations, lap joints, penetrations, and corners
Cementitious	Thoroseal from Thoro System Products	Easy to use, readily available	No elongation; will not accommodate joint or crack movement	Use acrylic additive for better bonding and durability
Bentonite Clay	Volclay panels from Colloid Environmental Technologies	Nonhazardous, nonpolluting, easy and quick to apply; can go on at low temperatures	Cannot be inspected for integrity (seal forms after backfilling)	"Pumped-in" bentonite retrofits are of dubious value

Availability and installation methods of waterproofing materials vary widely. While waterproofing will resist standing water in occasional extreme situations, no waterproofing system is designed to work without proper foundation drainage.

Drainage

Perimeter Foundation Drains

Every foundation below grade should be equipped with an exterior perimeter drain. Always work out a drainage plan before digging to locate cleanout and daylight locations of perimeter footing drains (**Figure 96**).

Perimeter foundation drainage must always be planned in conjunction with well-draining backfill (see "Soil Drainage," page 6, and "Backfill," page 109).

Placing Footing Drains

Place drain "tile" — typically 4-in. Schedule-C PVC or ABS pipe — with the holes down on a bed of gravel.

The gravel surrounding the drain should be wrapped with a geotextile, or filter fabric, to keep fine particles from clogging the drain tile.

Place drain tile straight and level, or with a slight pitch toward the exit. Do not attempt to create a pitch when

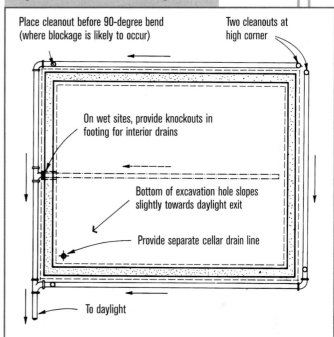

Figure 96. Perimeter Drainage Plan

Place cleanout before 90-degree bend (where blockage is likely to occur)

Two cleanouts at high corner

On wet sites, provide knockouts in footing for interior drains

Bottom of excavation hole slopes slightly towards daylight exit

Provide separate cellar drain line

To daylight

Plan drainage, including cleanout and daylight locations, before digging. On wet sites, plan on knockouts through the footing to connect to a drain under the slab.

using flexible drain tile, because undulations in the level can cause clogging. Flexible drain pipe should be placed on the footing shelf to prevent dips and sags (**Figure 98**, page 107). In either case, perimeter drain pipe should never

Figure 97. Interior Sump Basket

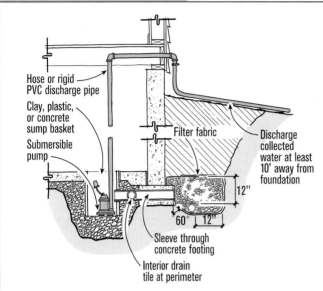

Hose or rigid PVC discharge pipe

Clay, plastic, or concrete sump basket

Submersible pump

Filter fabric

Discharge collected water at least 10' away from foundation

12"

60° 12"

Sleeve through concrete footing

Interior drain tile at perimeter

An interior sump basket picks up excess water flowing through sleeves in the footing. A submersible pump discharges the water at ground level away from the foundation.

be above the surface of the slab.

Tile should drain to daylight. If this is not possible, install a sump basket and a sump pump that discharges above ground away from the building (**Figure 97**).

Drainage Forms

Perimeter drainage can be provided with stay-in-place footing forms, such as Form-A-Drain®, to ensure a level perimeter drain. These systems usually provide a larger capacity than typical foundation pipe systems.

Surface Drainage

While perimeter drainage can handle water migrating through the soil, it may not be enough to handle a heavy run-off of surface water. The first line of defense against basement water problems should be handled at the surface.

Sloped Grade

The finish grade around the house should slope away from the foundation at the rate of $1/2$ to 1 in. per ft. for 6 to 10 ft. A 2- to 4-in. cap of silty-clay material — sometimes called a ground cap — will keep runoff from percolating down through the backfill. Better yet, use concrete or paver sidewalks sloped away from the house, or shallow subsurface drain pipes (**Figure 99**).

Make sure to properly compact backfill as you place it; otherwise, the soil will settle over time and create a slope draining toward the house (see "Backfill," page 109).

Gutter Downspouts

Use gutters and downspouts to divert roof runoff away from the foundation perimeter. If leaders dump out right next to the house they will concentrate

Figure 98. Placing Footing Drains

Pipe Even with Top of Footing

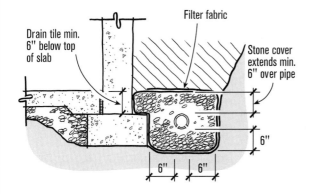

Filter fabric

Drain tile min. 6" below top of slab

Stone cover extends min. 6" over pipe

6"

6" | 6"

Pipe Below Footing

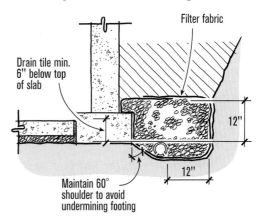

Filter fabric

Drain tile min. 6" below top of slab

12"

12"

Maintain 60° shoulder to avoid undermining footing

Pipe at Bottom of Footing

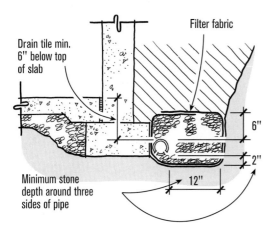

Filter fabric

Drain tile min. 6" below top of slab

6"

2"

Minimum stone depth around three sides of pipe

12"

Pipe Resting on Footing

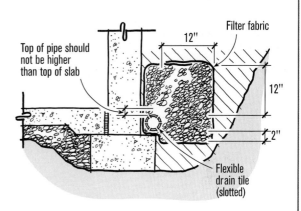

Filter fabric

12"

Top of pipe should not be higher than top of slab

12"

2"

Flexible drain tile (slotted)

The best location for rigid drain pipe is alongside the footing **(at left, top and bottom)**. Ideally, the drain should be at least 6 in. below the top of the slab and always covered by at least 6 in. of stone. If tile is placed below the footing, do not place it too close to the footing or water may undermine the footing **(at right, top)**. To keep flexible drain pipe from developing low spots, place it on top of the footings, making sure that the top of the pipe is not higher than the top of the interior slab and that it is covered by a 12-in.-deep bed of stone **(at right, bottom)**.

the problem in a smaller area. Extend downspout leaders 10 ft. away from foundation, or provide a sump basket and subsurface drain at the bottom of the downspout (**Figure 100**).

The Essential Guide to Foundations

Figure 99. Surface Drainage Without Gutters

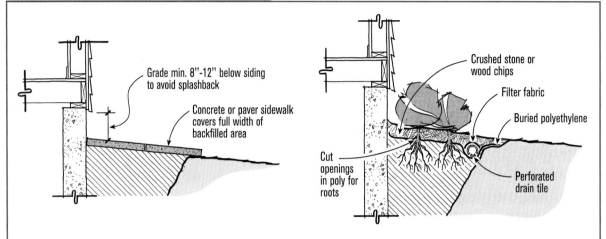

A properly sloped concrete or paver sidewalk will reduce the amount of runoff that percolates through the backfill **(left)**. Where perimeter plantings are used to landscape, improve drainage by burying a sheet of polyethylene below the plant bed, with openings cut out for roots **(right)**.

Figure 100. Channeling Gutter Discharge

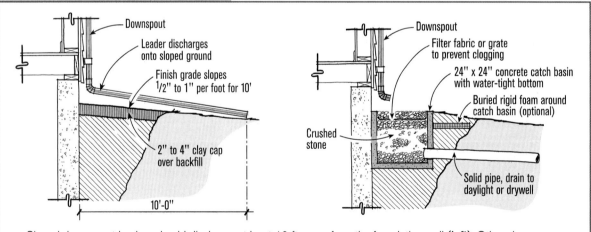

Sloped downspout leaders should discharge at least 10 ft. away from the foundation wall **(left)**. Otherwise, downspouts should discharge into a catch basin **(right)**.

Backfill

Bracing Before Backfill

Backfill should be placed only after the floor framing has been completed to brace the top of the foundation wall against the backfill load. If this is not possible, provide temporary foundation bracing, as shown in **Figure 101**.

Placing Backfill

Careful backfilling helps prevent foundation damage and soil settlement. Backfill only with well-draining granular fill (see "Drainage," pages 105-108).

Minimum Backfill Amount

Place the granular backfill in the zone from footing to near grade, widening to a minimum 30-degree angle from the footing up **(Figure 102)**.

Figure 101. Temporary Foundation Bracing

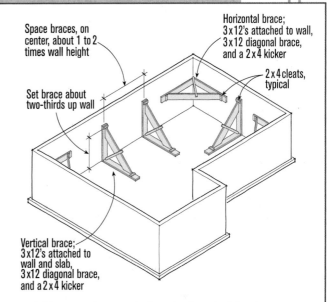

Space braces, on center, about 1 to 2 times wall height

Set brace about two-thirds up wall

Horizontal brace; 3 x 12's attached to wall, 3 x 12 diagonal brace, and a 2 x 4 kicker

2 x 4 cleats, typical

Vertical brace; 3 x 12's attached to wall and slab, 3 x 12 diagonal brace, and a 2 x 4 kicker

If backfilling must be done before the floor deck has been framed, install temporary foundation bracing. Set braces at about two-thirds the wall height and space braces apart about one to two times the wall height.

Figure 102. Backfilling Foundation Walls

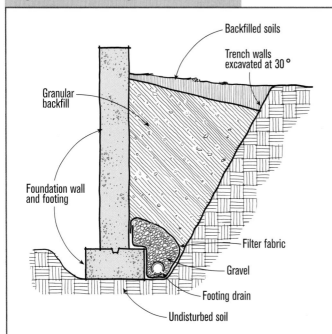

Backfilled soils

Trench walls excavated at 30°

Granular backfill

Foundation wall and footing

Filter fabric

Gravel

Footing drain

Undisturbed soil

If a foundation has not been excavated at least 3- to 4-ft. beyond the footing (see "Excavating Foundation Holes," page 13), widen the cut to at least 30 degrees from the base of the footing before placing backfill.

Foundation Backfill Checklist

- Use coarse granular material. Sandy or gravelly soils make the best back-fill.

- Compact the backfill. Place and compact the backfill in 6-in. lifts. Use hand compactors near the foundation, not machinery (see "Compacting Soil," page 10). Uniform-graded gravel is largely self-compacting, but sandy, silty, or clay soils will settle if not compacted.

- Slope final grade away from foundation. A minimum pitch of 6 in. in 10 ft. will direct surface water away from the foundation. For added insurance against settling, build final grade up deeper and at a steeper slope so it will still slope away from foundation after settlement. For additional drainage details, see "Drainage," pages 105-108.

Insulation

Insulating Foundation Walls

Foundation walls give up a significant amount of heat. Insulate poured-concrete and block foundation walls with a minimum of 1 in. of extruded polystyrene insulation. Expanded polystyrene (EPS), polyisocyanurate, and polyurethane rigid insulations are not recommended for below-grade applications.

Cold-Climate Foundation Insulation

Install insulation running the full height of the foundation wall. In cold-climates, "taper" exterior foundation insulation as follows:

- Install 1-in.-thick 2x8-ft. tongue-and-groove sheets vertically from footing to sill plate.

- Next, place a second layer of half-sheets (2x4-ft.) extending down 4 ft. with joints offset.

- Follow with a third layer of 2x8 sheets running horizontally across the top of the foundation.

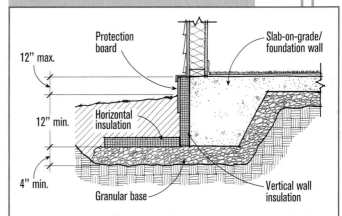

Figure 103. Shallow Foundation Insulation

12" max.

Protection board

Slab-on-grade/foundation wall

12" min.

Horizontal insulation

4" min.

Granular base

Vertical wall insulation

In a frost-protected foundation, foam insulation, rather than soil depth, keeps the soil at the footing from freezing. In mild climates, code requires only perimeter insulation projecting at least 24 in. to protect subslab soils from freezing and heaving.

Insulation Protection

Protect vertical insulation on the exterior of foundation walls with $3/8$- or $1/2$-in. pressure-treated plywood or a parging coat of Type M or S mortar applied over expanded-wire metal lath.

Figure 104. Minimum Insulation Requirements for Frost-Protected Foundations Under Heated Buildings

Heating Degree Days (°F days)	Vertical Insulation Min. R-Value*	Horizontal Insulation Min. R-Value*		Horizontal Insulation Dimensions per plan view (in.)		
		along walls	at corners	A	B	C
1,500 or less	4.5	not required	not required	not required	not required	not required
2,000	5.6	not required	not required	not required	not required	not required
2,500	6.7	1.7	4.9	12	24	40
3,000	7.9	6.5	8.6	12	24	40
3,500	9.0	8.0	11.2	24	30	60
4,000	10.1	10.5	13.1	24	36	60

* Note: Use the following R-values to determine insulation thicknesses required for this application:
Type II expanded polystyrene: 2.4R per inch.
Type IV, Type VI, and Type X extruded polystyrene: 4.5R per inch.
Type IX expanded polystyrene: 3.2R per inch.
Type X extruded polystyrene: 4.5R per inch.

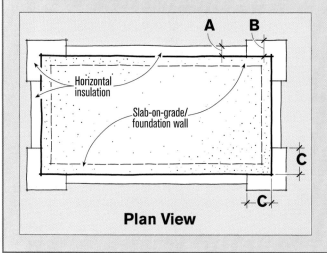

Plan View

Shallow foundations for heated buildings require insulation for protection against frost damage. Some state energy conservation standards may require greater values than those shown in the table above. Interpolation between values is permissible.

Adapted from 2000 International Residential Code

Frost-Protected Shallow Foundations

In cold climates, footings traditionally have been built below the maximum frost penetration depth (as deep as 5 ft. in the far north). However, codes now allow builders to use shallow footings or slabs-on-grade in any climate, as long as the soil under and around the foundation is protected from freezing with rigid insulating foam.

Horizontal Insulation for Structural Slabs

Insulation placement varies depending on whether the structure is heated or unheated:

- In mild climates, heated structures will need only vertical insulation along the edge of a structural slab.

- In colder areas, wing insulation is required, especially at the corners (**Figure 103**, page 111). Vertical and wing insulation specifications for the heated frost-protected shallow foundation are shown in **Figure 104**.

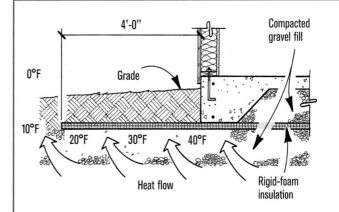

Figure 105. Insulation for Unheated Garage

For unheated slabs-on-grade, high-compression foam is placed under the entire slab to retain ground heat. The insulation must extend horizontally 4 ft. beyond the footing.

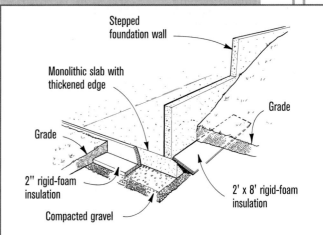

Figure 106. Insulating Walk-Out Basements

Insulate walk-out basement foundations with foam to avoid having to step down the excavation. A 2x8-ft. length of foam board protects the footing of the main wall at the corner where the backfill is shallow.

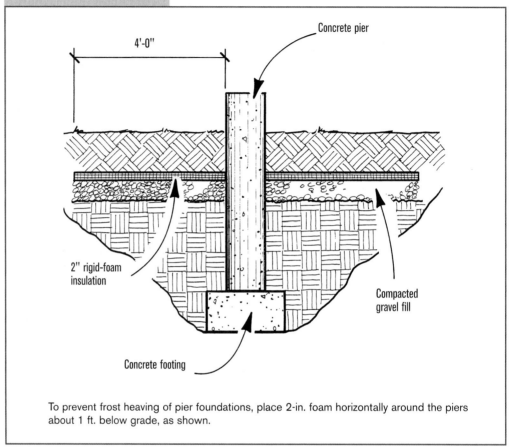

Figure 107. Insulating Piers

4'-0"

Concrete pier

2" rigid-foam insulation

Compacted gravel fill

Concrete footing

To prevent frost heaving of pier foundations, place 2-in. foam horizontally around the piers about 1 ft. below grade, as shown.

Protection for Horizontal Insulation

By code, horizontal insulation placed less than 12 in. below grade must be protected by a layer of concrete, asphalt paving, cementitious board, or pressure-treated plywood.

Perimeter Drainage

Slope finish grade at least 4 in. per 10 ft. In clay and silt-laden native soils, the soil beneath horizontal insulation should be backfilled with a well-compacted granular fill and perimeter drainage should be installed that drains to daylight (see "Drainage," page 105).

Frost-Protected Shallow Garage Foundations

An unheated structure, such as a detached garage, needs continuous insulation under the entire slab, extending out beyond the perimeter (**Figure 105**, page 113). Since there is no building heat to capture, this insulation is intended to prevent earth heat from escaping.

Foam for Frost-Protected Shallow Foundations

In this design, the footing and slab are bearing on the foam. By code, the foam used for frost-protected slabs must have a density of 2 lbs. per cu. ft. (See "Note" in **Figure 104**, page 112 for allowable Types.) Most expanded foam stocked by lumberyards is only 3/4-lb. or 1-lb. density and lacks sufficient compressive strength. High-compression foam usually needs to be special-ordered.

Insulation for Walkout Basements

The principle of frost protection can also be applied to special cases where foundation elements are vulnerable to frost, such as walkout basements (**Figure 106**, page 113). In these cases, carefully placed insulation can prevent frost action from damaging or moving structural elements.

Insulation for Piers

In some soils, even a 48-in.-deep post footing will sometimes be heaved up by frost. Post-and-pier foundations for decks and porches can be frost-proofed, using a 4-ft. strip of foam around post footings to keep the ground below from freezing (**Figure 107**).

Radon Abatement

Radon is a naturally occurring radioactive gas that is known to cause cancer in high doses. The risk associated with radon in residences remains uncertain, but the Environmental Protection Agency has recommended that every existing home be tested for radon and that action be taken if the test shows radon concentrations greater than 4.0 picocuries/liter of air.

Check Local Sources

The EPA also recommends that new homes be built with radon-resistant elements (**Figure 108**). This recommendation has been adopted as

Figure 108. Radon Elimination Strategies

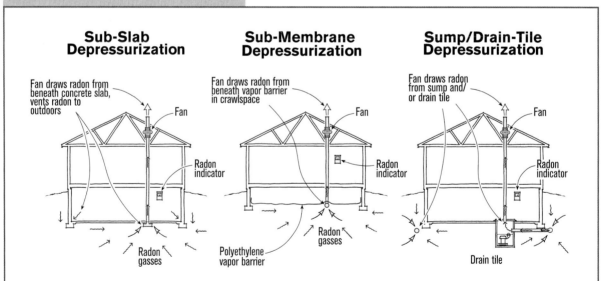

Different strategies for venting radon are required for different foundations: Houses with basements (left), houses with crawlspaces (center), and basements or slabs with sump chambers (right).

a requirement by some codes. These precautions are more important in areas where higher concentrations of radioactive materials are present in local rock. Check with state public health and environmental agencies about testing and risks in your area.

Subslab Poly

The EPA-recommended details for radon abatement call for poly to be placed above the gravel subbase and below the slab. Placing concrete directly on plastic can contribute to slab cracking due to uneven shrinkage and curling. For that reason, consider putting a layer of damp compacted sand above the poly before placing the concrete (see "Subslab Vapor Barriers," page 91).

Critical Construction Details

The EPA recommends the following system to prevent radon from entering basements and to conduct radon from below the slab to the outdoors:

- **Subslab:** Place gas-permeable layer (4-in. layer of clean gravel).

- **In basements:** Plastic sheeting should be placed on top of gravel sub-base and under slab.

- **In crawlspaces:** The sheeting is placed over the crawlspace floor.

- **Seal and caulk** all cracks, joints, or penetrations.

- **Use 3- or 4-in. PVC vent stack** from sub-slab to above roof. Mark this clearly so plumbers won't mistake it for a drain vent.

- **In attics:** Supply a junction box for power in case homeowners choose to install a powered vent fan.